# FRANK TALK
## ON OUR
# ROTARY
# FOUNDATION

FRANK J. DEVLYN   Rotary International President, 2000-2001
Chairman, 2005-2006 Rotary Foundation

and **David C. Forward,** Author, A Century of Service: The Story of Rotary International

# FRANK TALK
## ON OUR
# ROTARY
# FOUNDATION

**FRANK J. DEVLYN** Rotary International President, 2000-2001
Chairman, 2005-2006 Rotary Foundation

and **David C. Forward,** Author, A Century of Service: The Story of Rotary International

Reach*Forward* Publishing
www.Reach*Forward*.com

FRANK TALK on Our Rotary Foundation

For information address:
ReachForward Publishing
14 West Lake Ave.
Medford, NJ 08055-3429 USA
1-856-988-1738

ROTARY®,  , and are trademarks of Rotary
International. Used with permission.

Printed in the United States of America
Cover Photo by Alyce Henson. Used with permission.
Cover design and layout: Ad Graphics, Inc., Tulsa, OK

This book is not an official publication of Rotary International.

*FRANK TALK on Our Rotary Foundation* may be purchased individually for $12.95 or at substantial discounts for bulk orders
of 10 or more copies. Rates are quoted in US funds and do not
include shipping and handling.

For more information see the Resource Center at:
www.ReachForward.com
www.FrankTalkBooks.com

ISBN: 0-9711030-5-4

*To my wife and partner in Rotary, Gloria Rita. Without her support, I could never have dedicated the passion and the time I have given to Rotary. Thanks to Gloria Rita, we have both made Rotary an important part of our lives*

*– Frank*

# ACKNOWLEDGMENTS

The authors wish to extend their personal thanks to so many people who have contributed their time, advice, and experiences to make this book possible. At the risk of unwittingly offending some whose names we may have overlooked, they especially thank Ann Fleming, Chris Forward, Luis Giay, Hogie Hansen, and John Osterlund for their help.

This book is written to honor all those Rotarians who contribute to The Rotary Foundation on an annual basis and whose consistent support for our Foundation has made dreams come true all over the world. We especially want to recognize those Rotarians who are Paul Harris Fellows, Benefactors, and Paul Harris Society, Bequest Society, and Arch Klumph Society members. Your support is helping our Foundation become a world recognized premier Foundation

# CONTENTS

# About Frank Devlyn

In the world of Rotary, Frank Devlyn is recognized as being one of the most sought-out speakers, constantly in demand for Rotary conferences and events.

His background gives good reason why he is considered by so many to be such a unique, successful leader. Raised on the border between México and the United States, Frank proudly describes himself as bicultural. "As a youngster and student, I spent time in both countries every day," he says. "Home was in Juarez, México, where my mother's family came from, and I went to school in El Paso, Texas. I was immersed equally in both cultures every day of my life."

Frank's father, Frank Devlyn, Sr., a World War I veteran of Irish descent, came from a small town near Chicago, Illinois. Frank, Sr., was an optometrist, as is Frank's mother, Nelva. After they married, they moved to Nelva's northern México hometown of Juarez, the country's largest border city, and opened a small optical shop. Frank grew up in the family business and worked in the store every day after school. At age nine, he made his first pair of eyeglasses.

When Frank turned 22, his father died. By that time, the Devlyns had opened their seventh optical shop. Frank then had to lead the family business with the help of his mother and two younger brothers. In both hard times and good, the Devlyn chain of optical stores has continued to expand. Today Devlyn Optical Group has more than 500 stores and is the largest retail optical company in Latin America, with branches in México, Guatemala, El Salvador, Honduras, and the Dominican Republic. The company also wholesales, distributes, and manufactures a variety of optical and ophthalmic products through Latin America.

As testament to his prodigious networking ability, Frank sits on the boards of numerous national and international groups. He is frequently asked to serve in a public capacity and it is not uncommon to see Frank being interviewed by the media, Mexican government, or by organizations representing private enterprise seeking his advice.

He joined the three-week old Rotary Club of Anáhuac in Mexico City when he was 29. "I doubt, at that time, whether the larger clubs in town would have invited a businessman of my age." He served as the club's third president. Frank describes joining Rotary as "a turning point in my life," and he brought to Rotary the same energy, determination and forward thinking that were hallmarks of his business career.

His blueprint for Rotary in his 2000-01 presidential year was characteristically ambitious. To help Rotarians accomplish his goals and give meaning and life to the theme of *Create Awareness—Take Action*, Frank appointed 20 task forces. Each one focused on work that Rotary clubs worldwide were doing, he says. Each one had "a specific reason for being," well-defined goals and a plan of action.

Frank and Gloria Rita, his wife of 40 years, have three daughters—Melanie Devlyn-Perez (wife of Juan Carlos Pérez Collado) Stephanie Devlyn-Alcocer (Luis Alcocer Lamm) and Jennifer Devlyn-Maccise (Luis Maccise Uribe)—and nine grandchildren: Alexia, Luis, Carlos Francisco, Jennifer, Pablo, Michelle, and triplets Elena, Viviana, and Luis. Gloria Rita has been Frank's partner in Rotary as in life, joining him at Rotary functions at all levels. For that reason, she was made an honorary Rotarian by Frank's Mexico City—Anahuac Club.

Frank's is a true Rotarian family.

- Frank's mother Nelva, a former "woman of the year" of Juarez, was also named an Honorary Rotarian for her civic professional work by the Juarez Integra Rotary Club.

- His brother, Jesse, another optical entrepreneur, is general director of the Devlyn Optical Group. A member of the Rotary Club of San Rafael, Mexico City, Jesse is well known to Rotarians worldwide and has served as district governor, committee and task force member, International Assembly discussion leader, and sergeant-at-arms at international assemblies and conventions.

- Another brother, Patrick, general manager of the Devlyn Group, is a past president of his Rotary club and a GSE team leader and board member of the Rotary Eyecare Fellowship beside being a well-known motivational speaker on personal development.

- A sister, Ethel Devlyn-Gaspar de Alba (Mario, her husband, is a Rotarian in El Paso, Texas.)

- Another brother, Gordon, is a Rotarian in Elk Grove Village, Illinois.

This brief synopsis illustrates Frank Devlyn's commitment to business excellence and community involvement:

- President and CEO of the Devlyn Optical Group of México.
- Past president of the:

▲ Optometrist and Opticians Association of México,

▲ Optical Manufacturers Section of the National Chamber of Industries of México,

▲ Hearing Aid Distributors Association of Mexico,

▲ Toastmasters Club of Mexico City,

▲ and of the National Contact Lens Manufacturing Association.

- Educated in El Paso, Texas, and Mexico City. A proud alumnus of the University of Texas at El Paso and the I.P.A.D.E. business school in México City.

- Graduate of the School of Optometry of the Mexican Association of Optometrists.

- Regional board member of a leading Mexican bank, Banamex (Citicorp Group).

- Past member of the international board of Goodwill Industries International.

- Board Member of Funsalud—One of Mexico's leading health-related foundations.

- Treasurer of the Tuberculosis and Lung Association of México.

- Past Member of the board of directors of the Mexican Red Cross.

- President of México's Vecino Vigilante initiative, a neighborhood watch program sponsored by Rotary clubs, and a broad group of organizations collectively known as "México United Against Crime."

- Board Member of Mexico's "Centro Mexicano Para la Filantropía" which unites Mexico's most reputable philanthropic organizations.

- Past Advisory Board member of The Wheelchair Foundation.

- Past Board member of The Order of Malta in Mexico.

- Founding editor and director of the Rotary regional magazine, Rotarismo en México.

- Governor of District 4170 in 1977-78.

- R.I. director for 1986-88.

- President of Rotary International for 2000-2001.

- Trustee of The Rotary Foundation of R.I. for 1996-98 and 2002-2006.

- Chairman, The Rotary Foundation Board of Trustees, 2005-2006.

- Chairman, Avoidable Blindness Task Force, 2001-2003.

- Avoidable Blindness Advisor for R.I.'s Health Concerns Task Force 2003-2004.

- Recipient of The Rotary Foundation's Distinguished Service Award and its Citation for Meritorious Service for his support of its international humanitarian and educational programs.

- Awarded the Medal of Honor of the México City Chamber of Commerce by Vicente Fox, President of Mexico in 2001.

- Named honorary citizen in numerous cities worldwide where he has represented Rotary.

- Presented a honorary doctorate in business administration by the prestigious Hanyang University of Korea in 2005.

# About David C. Forward

David C. Forward was born and educated in England before moving to the United States in 1972. He is a successful real estate broker in Southern New Jersey and a much-demanded speaker at Rotary district conferences and PETS. He has frequently been featured in the national and international media, including ABC TV and the BBC.

David is a prolific writer, and has written eight books, including:

- *Heroes After Hours*
- *Sales SuperStars*
- *The Essential Guide to the Short-Term Mission Trip*
- *DUH! Lessons in Employee Motivation that Every Business Should Learn*
- *DUH! Lessons in Customer Service that every Business Should Learn*
- *DUH! Lessons in Leadership that every Business Should Learn(in preparation)*

David co-authored *Frank Talk, Frank Talk II,* and *Frank Talk on Our Rotary Foundation* with R.I. President Frank J. Devlyn, and they became the best-selling books in Rotary history, with more than 125,000 books distributed in eight languages. In 2004, R.I. released *A Century of Service: the Story of Rotary International,* which David wrote.

A Rotarian since 1978, he served in many club and district leadership positions and is now an honorary member of the Rotary Club of San Francisco. David

Forward is a Major Donor to The Rotary Foundation and was awarded the Citation for Meritorious Service for his work as district chairman of the PolioPlus Committee. In addition to his volunteer work in Rotary, David is an elder in his church, and is voluntary president of International Children's Aid Foundation, a ministry that assists orphaned children in Romania. In 2005, the 1.3-million-member National Association of Realtors named David national winner of its Good Neighbor Award for his volunteerism.

After 27 years as a Rotarian in a traditional club, David joined the Rotary eClub One in 2006.

# FOREWORD

# Frank Talk *Three?*

In March 2001, then-Rotary International President Frank J. Devlyn decided to write a book. When he enlisted author David C. Forward to help, David asked the most basic question: *What are your objectives for such a book?* With barely a moment's hesitation, Frank replied, "I want to leave a legacy for Rotary, long after I have left the office as President."

Rotary had experienced either flat, or in some regions, a decline in membership in the years immediately prior to 2000. The more the two men talked, the more two things became evident to the author: First, Frank refined his objectives to make membership growth his primary goal of the book project, and second, he was to use his own money—not Rotary International's—to pay for its production. He then vowed that all profits from sales would go to The Rotary Foundation. Worthy aspirations indeed, thought David.

And so the story began to take shape of Frank's flight cancellation and his re-routing onto a train. During that journey, he began chatting with three strangers in the same compartment. They were people who fit the broad demographics of people we would like to bring into Rotary. Sue, a professional entrepreneur; Bob, a young man in the computer industry who until then had placed his priorities in all the wrong places, and Duncan, a man just entering early retirement who had grown up with the "give back" ethic and who now had ample time and resources to do so. The authors thought back to all the people they had invited to join Rotary over the years and realized they could categorize almost all the excuses people gave them into five or six reasons. So the book was structured so that each time Frank invited one of his traveling companions to join Rotary, they came up with one of these objections. Frank then used compelling arguments to overcome those objections. By the end of their trip, all three of them agreed to consider joining Rotary.

*Frank Talk* went on to become the fastest-selling book in Rotary history and was translated into Spanish, Portuguese, Arabic, Mandarin, Turkish, Korean, and Vietnamese. Literally thousands of Rotary clubs and individual Rotarians bought—and continue to buy—the book both for their own members and also to give as a gift to guest speakers, potential members, and community leaders to explain who they were and why they meet and do such good work around town every week.

However, as David came to realize, Frank Devlyn is not a "one book kind of guy!" He realized that while membership development is of critical importance to Rotary, many new members leave within a year or two because they do not feel their clubs have what was promised to them. Thus, the idea was born for a second book, appropriately called *Frank Talk II*, which dealt with membership retention and how to energize a Rotary Club.

In the narrative, Frank Devlyn, now a Past Rotary International President, attends the district conference of the very district where Sue, Bob, and Duncan belong. He is shocked to discover that Bob has all-but dropped out of Rotary and Sue, while incoming club president, has developed serious frustrations and misgivings about her club and the whole Rotary experience. The book was written as a collage of real-world vignettes that the two writers and many Rotarians shared from their many years of Rotary membership. Rotary, after all, is composed of ordinary human beings, and the same shortcomings that cause us to become disillusioned with friends, workplaces, community organizations, and places of worship can often be found in the local Rotary club.

Frank gave the three Rotarians numerous ideas on how to stay motivated themselves and how to make their Rotary clubs more energetic, on how to make their service more dynamic and effective, and how to bypass the negative attitudes some members of their clubs always seemed to have. Once again, *Frank Talk II* went into multiple languages and several reprints and sold thousands of copies all over the world.

In 2005-2006, Frank Devlyn served as Chairman of the Board of Trustees of The Rotary Foundation. And you guessed it: He decided to write another book!

Frank often asked audiences where he was speaking what they thought he should name his next book after *Frank Talk II*. They usually yelled out "Frank Talk Three!" It was after such occasions that his wife Gloria Rita would recommend it be called *Frank Talks Too Much*, or his brother Pat would advise it be titled, *Pat Listens!* But all along, Frank's serious motive was to introduce a book, again co-authored by David C. Forward, to the Rotary world that dealt with his passion for making The Rotary Foundation a priority to all Rotarians.

*Frank Talk on Our Rotary Foundation* picks up the same thread from the previous books. His objective with this book was to make more Rotarians more involved with The Rotary Foundation. That means more involved as hands-on volunteers, and more involved as financial contributors to the Foundation. The same three characters the reader has met before are again featured in the third book, but what a difference the ensuing three years have made! They could not be more different from the last time Frank met them. Each of them has become actively involved in Rotary's humanitarian work and tells inspiring stories of what they have experienced. The truism in Rotary is that the more people are involved with The Rotary Foundation's work, the more generous they usually are toward it.

Each of the stories or their concepts in this book are true, although sometimes certain details have been changed to avoid giving one person or one country too much exposure. When Frank speaks, he cites his own experiences of projects he has seen and Rotarians he has met who have made The Rotary Foundation a major focus of their benevolence commitment. As we were preparing to write the book, Frank and David once again sought editorial contributions from their wide circle of Rotary friends on why they have supported The Rotary Foundation, and many of those testimonies are included in the following pages. Other inspiring real-life anecdotes were gleaned from the pages of *The Rotarian* or annual reports of The Rotary Foundation. Yet more stories were discovered from David's interviews with Rotary Foundation staff and his own field work and from his numerous speaking engagements at PETS and district conferences around the Rotary world. We did not have to look far to find a multitude of inspiring stories and inspiring Rotarians who are tirelessly working to make *their* Foundation a life-changing dynamic body.

In the following pages, you will find many things. In its simplest form, one could consider this book a series of nice stories, easy to digest and hopefully making the reader feel good about Rotary and their Foundation. However, if that is all you take away from this book, the authors will have failed. The real reason they have written it is to ramp up _your_ involvement— yes, _you who are reading this right now!_—in The Rotary Foundation. Can you take a week or a month to become a Rotary volunteer sometime soon? Will you? Can you persuade your Rotary club to host a GSE team this year, or sponsor an Ambassadorial Scholar? Will you research the needs for Matching Grants and work with your friends in Rotary to fund one of them? Can you include The Rotary Foundation in your charitable giving budget, both in annual giving and in your estate plan?

One could argue that with such a record of accomplishment of success in solving seemingly insoluble problems around the world that true Rotarians could not possibly ignore The Rotary Foundation. So why do quite a large number of members not give to their Foundation on an annual basis? There are perhaps two reasons: they do not have 'top-of-mind awareness' of the needs and opportunities, and they are not asked to give.

This book is intended to provide you with a series of compelling stories that illustrate the very essence of The Rotary Foundation—and it is our hope that you will then feel empowered to 'make the ask.' People do not give to organizations; they give to causes and people who touch their senses. Please carry the torch for The Rotary Foundation—for _YOUR_ Rotary Foundation—by making the personal commitment to be better supporters from this moment on, and then to enlist your family, friends, associates, and fellow

Rotarians to join the team by following your leadership example.

Why?

How do you put a price tag on saving a woman or child from walking three miles each way to carry water every day? Now multiply that by two hundred in the village, because The Rotary Foundation gave them a much-needed clean-water well.

How do you put a price tag on saving one life from malaria or helping a person not to have to endure the agony of almost dying and losing their income for months? Your Rotary Foundation is helping stop the spread of malaria by providing mosquito nets to communities throughout Africa—where one million die from malaria every year.

How do you count the cost of giving an older person a new lease on life through one of the thousands of heart pacemakers a Rotary Foundation 3-H Grant gave to Heartbeat International?

What is the impact in your district when a member returns from being a Rotary volunteer in another country and relates what he or she has seen—because you supported a Rotary Foundation Volunteer Service Grant?

How can you place a value on the long-term benefit to a group of impoverished women in Honduras—where a Rotary Foundation Matching Grant provided microcredit loans for them to obtain sewing machines to start their own cottage businesses?

How do you measure the cost of an Ambassadorial Scholar who has experienced Rotary generosity first hand?

How do you put a price tag on the training of a Rotary Peace and Conflict Resolution Scholar who some day just might help two countries avoid going to war?

We hope you read every word in this book and when you are finished, feel as proud of The Rotary Foundation and of our fellow Rotary volunteers who are in the trenches changing lives every day, and of the generous donors who make it all possible.

Then we hope you will accept our invitation to the table of service to humankind that has been set by Our Rotary Foundation: we are holding a place for you right now!

– Frank J. Devlyn
– David C. Forward

For indigent people living in San Pablo City, Philippines, access to health care is hampered by high costs, lack of awareness of existing services, and other barriers.

"A day's pay is just enough for a day of food, [with nothing] for other needs" observed Dr. Noel Alidio, project coordinator and a member of the Rotary Club of San Pablo City. "Some malnourished children are too weak to go to school. They [also] suffer from pneumonia, diarrheal diseases, skin infections, infestations. Adults are also prone to malnutrition, tuberculosis, and other chronic illnesses."

Alidio and several of his fellow club members volunteer regularly at a clinic sponsored by his club. Aided by a Rotary Foundation Matching Grant, the Rotary clubs of San Pablo City and Crows Nest, New South Wales, Australia, teamed up to provide the clinic with badly needed medicines and hepatitis B vaccine.

"The clinic project has made health care delivery accessible to these people," said Alidio. "Patients are now more equipped to manage their medical problems with proper knowledge and guidance."

## CHAPTER 1

# Hello Again!

"**F**rank!" I cannot believe it! You haven't changed a bit." The voice—and the exuberant greeting—were unmistakable.

"Sue!" I exclaimed. "You look wonderful. It was *so* nice of you to come all the way out to the airport to meet me. I'm very sorry the flight was late."

"That's not a problem," she replied. "I got a chance to catch up on some paperwork and returned all my phone calls. Anyway, at least *this* time the flight did finally operate—unlike our first meeting, when the airport shut down."

"That's right," I agreed, remembering that foggy morning six years earlier when I had been forced to take a train to my final destination after my flight—and all others—was canceled. "But you know, Sue, if those airplanes had operated, we all would never have met on that train."

"Yes—and Bob, Duncan, and I would never have joined Rotary," she said, with a huge grin. "Here, let me carry your computer while you bring your other bag. The car is this way." We did not have far to go. As we walked, she explained that Phil Jefferson, the airport director, had recently joined her Rotary Club, and had given her access to the VIP parking spot just outside the baggage claim hall. Within five minutes, we were in her car and on the way to town.

As we settled into the center lane on the motorway, Sue's expression turned more serious. "Frank," she said, "I know that the moment we get to the conference, you will be mobbed by people...your adoring fans!" She flashed a mischievous smile at me. "So I want to take advantage of this time together to say 'Thank you.'"

"Thank you? Thank you for what?" I asked.

"For everything you've done for me. First, that morning on the train, you could have immersed your-self in work, read the newspaper, or listened to a CD. But instead, you took the time to tell us how we could enrich our lives—and improve the lives of others—by joining Rotary."

"But Sue, I was international president of Rotary at the time. If *I* would not do that, who in the world would have?"

"I know, I know," she continued. "In a way, get-ting *into* Rotary was easy. However, it was what came later that makes me so grateful to you. I was so demo-tivated by some of the people in my club who wanted to be members of a knife-and-fork fellowship, not a Rotary club, that I was on the point of leaving Rotary when I last met you."

I well remembered that meeting. I had represent-ed the then-president of Rotary International at the district conference, and had eaten dinner with Sue, Bob, and Duncan the night I arrived. Rather than a celebratory reunion, the occasion had begun more like a wake. Sue—and incoming club president—was close to resigning. Bob had already all-but dropped out. Only Duncan, a member of a different Rotary club, had given a positive report of his experiences. The entire evening had involved my suggestions of how they could ener-gize their members and refocus their clubs into truly service-minded, rather than self-minded groups.

"You threw down a challenge that night," she recalled. "And Bob and I accepted it. Looking back, I believe that was the weekend when, through your encouragement and the inspiration from the speakers at the district conference, we changed from being members of a Rotary club to being Rotarians."

"And Duncan?"

"He was already there!" We both laughed.

"Sounds like it's been quite a couple of years," I said.

"Three." She corrected me. "That conference was almost three years ago."

"Tell me about your Rotary journey in the past three years."

"Gosh, I don't think I have time before we get to the hotel," she said, with a sigh. "Well, here's the abbreviated version. The fact is, Frank, I came away from that district conference really motivated to energize my club when I became president. I had so many ideas that Bob and Duncan actually counseled me to tone down my plans a little. And they were right; no club president can do everything in one year."

That's true," I said. "I even went through the same realization when I became Rotary International president. So what *did* you focus on?"

"The Rotary Foundation," Sue answered. "I thought our members were already familiar with their opportunities to serve in the local community; we certainly are a very positive force for good in our town. Club fellowship was working well, but I surmised most members gave little or no support to The Rotary Foundation."

"Why do you think that is?"

"*Was*," she corrected me.

"Sorry, why do you think that *was*?"

"They just had no idea what the Foundation was all about. For years, various club Foundation chairs or presidents had weakly promoted The Rotary Foundation with announcements like, 'Well, folks, it's that time of the year again. Please consider a donation to The Rotary Foundation because October is Rotary Foundation month.' Give me a break! I was in the club almost three years and nobody had ever really told me what an incredible gift to the world The Rotary Foundation is. When I think back at all the missed opportunities our club—and thousands of other clubs—had, it makes me sick." She pointed her finger into her mouth to emphasize her point.

"You really feel strongly about this, don't you?" I asked.

"You bet I do!" she exclaimed. "Rotary is touching the lives of literally millions of people through our Foundation. However, imagine what we *could* have accomplished if just 25 percent of the Rotarians gave to their true potential. Imagine how many diseases could have been cured. Imagine how many mothers would not have watched their babies die due to malnutrition or unclean drinking water..." her voice trailed off as if she really was trying to imagine such a vision.

Several seconds of silence passed before I felt it appropriate to speak. "So what did you do differently in your year as club president?" I enquired.

> "Dream as if you'll live forever...
> Live as if you'll die today."
> – James Dean

"I decided to focus on The Rotary Foundation," she began. "I certainly did not forget our local community service, but our club had done very little for The Rotary Foundation. I asked myself, *Are we part of an international service organization, or not?* So I appointed a committee of people I trusted to be good communicators and several weeks before I took office, we spent a Sunday afternoon at my home—sort of a retreat. I had called The Rotary Foundation office in Evanston, Illinois, and they sent me a huge assortment of materials describing the work the Foundation does and the many ways people can help. However, even more importantly, they put me in touch with the Regional Rotary Foundation Coordinator for our area, and he became an enormously valuable and inspiring resource. That afternoon, we watched some incredibly moving stories on video. I remember one tape The Rotary Foundation sent me called One Blue Sky. Another inspiring resource was a nine-minute DVD from The Rotary Foundation. It really opened my eyes. We resolved to give a Rotary Foundation Minute at each of the 52 club meetings in my year.

"I believe that our first priority was to educate our members—to make them proud to be Rotarians. I also believe that the most convincing messengers are those who are already committed to the message. Therefore, at the end of our afternoon retreat, I invited each member of the committee to make a personal commitment to The Rotary Foundation. Every one of them did, pledging a total of $17,000 to The Rotary Foundation.

"We then divided the club into teams, and each member on my committee became a team captain. At first, we considered having a contest to see which team could raise the most money for The Rotary Foundation. But then we realized that was not such a good idea."

"Why not?" I asked.

"For several reasons. Firstly, benevolence should be encouraged based on one's personal ability to give. It would not be fair to reward one team that had an individual member able to write a large check, while passing over another team—whose members may have had more modest means—even though they may have given generously. Besides, I did not want it to be just about money. It is true that many Rotarians are very generous with their financial gifts, but I wanted to make them feel personally involved—even to have some hands-on experience with Rotary Foundation projects. I really believed—and still believe—that the more we can make Rotarians feel a *personal* connection with these programs, the more they will think of it not as *The* Rotary Foundation, but as *their* Rotary Foundation."

"Wow! That's pretty powerful thinking, Sue." I said. "I could not agree with you more. Now you've got me sitting on the edge of my seat...that was almost three years ago, so tell me, how did you do?"

She momentarily took her eyes off the road to flash me a quick smile. "Frank, it was an incredible year! This club, the very club I was thinking of quitting because it felt downright moribund, responded in truly amazing ways.

"Firstly, just before the year began, Bob—you remember Bob—was sent by his company on a month-long trip to their new computer center in Hyderabad, India. While there, he contacted local Rotarians who took him out to various projects that The Rotary Foundation was funding. So he returned with hundreds of photographs and amazingly moving stories about how we can make a difference by helping support these programs. People in the club were really moved by his compelling testimony.

"Oh, and while we're on the subject of people you know, Duncan was our district's Rotary Foundation chairman the year I was club president. He is such a nice person, and I wanted to support him; he sure was a wonderful resource for me. Anyway, he was gone for quite a while because he took an around-the-world trip."

I remembered Duncan had taken—not entirely voluntarily—early retirement from his job not long before we had met. "Well, he had worked hard all his life," I volunteered. "He had certainly earned a nice vacation."

"Yes, but this was no vacation, Frank," said Sue. "He cashed in some of those frequent flyer miles he had accumulated and took a trip around the world visiting—and volunteering—at Rotary Foundation work projects. He called it his 'vacation with a purpose.' You will hear him discuss it in his workshop tomorrow. Anyhow, he sent each club president in our district weekly e-mails filled with inspirational anecdotes of The Rotary Foundation in action—and I forwarded them to every member of my club.

"We also had a make-up visitor from Brazil who attended our club for several meetings while visiting his daughter. Many of our members got to know him quite well, and when he told us of the problems of a well-baby clinic his club had started in a very poor neighborhood in his city, we wanted to help. In fact, our members proposed launching a joint project with Jose's club. So we did.

"And do you know what made me the happiest, Frank? Three of those people were folks I had written off in my mind as 'do-nothing, knife-and-fork members'. It was the first sign to me that if we connect real needs with real Rotarians, amazing things can happen."

"You know, Sue, at the end of *A Century of Service*, the official history of Rotary's first one hundred years, the author pointed out that every program, every successful project, every ideal which helped Rotary become the world's leading service organization came not from the top down but from the grass roots up. That is what you witnessed. You tilled the soil, planted the seed, nurtured the first tentative sprouts—and it sounds like you reaped quite a harvest."

"I haven't even told you the half of it," she said, nodding affirmatively. "We sent two teams of volunteers on field trips. We hosted a Group Study Exchange team. We became involved with the Peace Scholar program. And, at the end of the year, our club, which had never given more than $12,000 to The Rotary Foundation in any previous year, turned in $51,000 in cash, and another $36,000 in pledges of future contributions."

"Sue, I cannot believe what I am hearing," I said. "I am so proud of you. Aren't you the one who told me on the train that you did not belong in Rotary because it was a 'boring old men's club'?"

"Oh, there are still some of them out there, Frank," she said. We both laughed.

"But seriously, Sue, you are exactly the person Rotary needs—and may I add, as chairman of The Rotary Foundation—you evidently are exactly the type of person The Rotary Foundation needs, too."

"Well, thank you Frank," she answered. "I really do appreciate those words. But truthfully, I feel a little guilty accepting them, because I am already so rewarded with the knowledge that in my own small way, I am making a difference in the world."

I was contemplating a response, when Sue spoke again: "Okay. We are here. Why don't you grab your bags from the back seat and we'll let the valet park the car."

We entered the large hotel, quickly checked in, and then Sue gave me an overview of what was to happen next. I was relieved to be offered the opportunity to go to my room without any meetings and to sleep off the effects of my long flight from Argentina. She explained that although she was now district Rotary Foundation chair, this weekend was a multi-district Rotary Foundation conference—the first of its kind I had heard of. They expected me to give an opening keynote address on Friday morning, and then the closing speech on Saturday. There would be several workshops on both days, on various topics concerning The Rotary Foundation.

As I followed, the bellhop into my room, I suddenly felt very tired. My final thoughts as I lay my head on the pillow were of the three people whom I had met on that foggy train ride. Three people with absolutely no knowledge of Rotary, nor the slightest interest in joining Rotary. Their arguments to such a suggestion had been entirely self-gratifying: *we do not have time...we will not like the other members...we do not want to spend the money...it might be boring for us.*

Nevertheless, they *did* join. Then, the last time I ran into them, two of the three were about to drop out—again because they were focusing on themselves. What a tragedy that would have been! Now look at them. They were motivated—and motivating others. They had touched the lives of countless desperately needy people, and were thrilled to have done so. Now, their lives had an entirely different focus: it was *outward*, on helping others.

What is it that Sue said? "We have changed from being members of a Rotary club to becoming Rotarians." Indeed, they had!

In many Latin American countries, children suffer serious burns from cooking and heating fires, fireworks, sunburn, and other accidental causes. In 1979, Dr. Jorge Rojas, of the Rotary Club of Santiago, Chile, founded Coaniquem (Corporation for the Aid of Burned Children) to provide free treatment and rehabilitation to burned children, help prevent accidental burns, and train health care professionals.

"We wanted to ensure equal treatment for every child, with no concern about a family's ability to pay," said Rojas. "Burn-related accidents occur at every level of society, and Coaniquem helps everyone who needs it."

A Health, Hunger and Humanity (3-H) project trained Rotarians, Rotaractors, Interactors, Rotary Community Corps, and others to carry out burn prevention campaigns in eight South American cities. It also rehabilitated child burn victims at Coaniquem's Santiago and Antofagasta treatment centers, and trained medical professionals in the eight cities in all phases of this specialized care. The two Chilean centers now enable Coaniquem to treat some 9,000 patients from 11 countries annually. A charitable foundation was established in the USA to extend support for Coaniquem after the end of 3-H funding.

Rotary clubs in several South American countries and District 5170 (California, USA) helped implement the 3-H project and continue to provide support. As a slogan of the Rotary Club of Asunción, Paraguay, states in promoting aid for burn victims: "Pain has no borders, neither does Rotary service."

# CHAPTER 2

# One
# Extraordinary Life

"**I** am here to tell you about one extraordinary life,"
I said. I paused for a good ten seconds, scanning
the audience slowly from right to left. There had to
be at least six hundred people out there for this, the
opening keynote address of Sue's multi-district Rotary Foundation conference. The longer the silence, the
more I felt their rapt attention.

"In all likelihood, it is the life of a man most of you
have never heard of."

Pause.

"In the annals of great men who have helped
change the course of human history, we might think
of Gandhi, or Dr. Martin Luther King, Jr., or Nelson
Mandela. But it is none of these."

I paused again.

"You may think I am going to talk about Paul Harris. But I am not."

I saw some quizzical looks from people in the
front row.

"I speak of a man who had all the cards stacked
against him. His name was Arch Klumph. Born in a
small town in Western Pennsylvania in 1869, his fam-

ily was desperately poor. There were no jobs in that rural mountainous area, so when he was still a child, the family moved to the booming industrial city of Cleveland. Even then, they could barely survive, and so, at the age of twelve, they sent young Archie out to work as an office boy for a lumber company.

"But this remarkable lad had a drive to succeed, and he took the initiative to enlist in night school. So every night after work, he then went to school— walking four miles because he could not afford the tram fare.

"His employer noticed this exceptional young man, and gradually gave him more responsibilities. When, a few years later, the company looked like it was going to fail, the owners asked Arch Klumph—still the teenager with boundless energy, initiative, and ideas—to take over as manager. And guess what? The company began to turn around. In fact, it did so well that he ultimately became CEO and bought the company—and Cuyahoga Lumber became the most successful firm of its type in the Midwest. Arch Klumph went on to own companies as diverse as Security Savings and Loan, Monticello Realty, and the Lake Steamship Company.

"This boy from the mountains of Pennsylvania taught himself how to play the flute at the age of eighteen, and three years later became a flutist for the Cleveland Symphony Orchestra, with which he remained for the next fourteen years.

"Now, you may be wondering, 'Why is Frank telling us about this interesting—but completely irrelevant—man. What does it have to do with me?'

"My Rotary friends, if it were not for Arch Klumph, none of us would be here today."

I paused again to let the words sink in.

"You see, soon after the Cleveland Rotary Club began in 1911, somebody invited Arch Klumph to become a member. They, too, recognized him as an amazing man, because they made him club president the very next year. In his final address as president of the Rotary Club of Cleveland, Klumph proposed 'an emergency fund should be built up which will enable the club in future years to do many things.' However, they ignored his proposal.

"Just four years after that, Arch Klumph became president of what we now know as Rotary International. He presided over the world's fastest-growing service organization at the height of the First World War. It was Arch Klumph who chaired the committee that led to a standard constitution and by-laws for all Rotary clubs. It was also Klumph's idea to divide Rotary into districts, to create the office of district governor, and to hold district conferences. Yet he never gave up on his strong belief that Rotary should create a trust fund to—as he put it: 'do good in the world.'

"By the end of his presidential year in 1917, he had become a strong advocate for this endowment fund, suggesting to audiences that Rotarians could contribute to it for 'charitable, educational, or other avenues of community progress.'

"But he carried the torch almost alone. Delegates to the annual convention that year in Atlanta—and members of the Board—gave Klumph's

> "If you love Rotary, you'll show it in at least three ways: by bringing in qualified new members, by helping Rotary change with the times, and by promoting and supporting Our Rotary Foundation."
> – Frank Devlyn

idea a polite response, but did nothing to make it a reality. A whole year passed with no further action. However, when the organizers of the 1918 Kansas City Convention realized they had $26.50 left over after paying all the bills, they designated it as the very first gift to Klumph's Rotary Endowment Fund.

"But Arch had hardly won his battle. For years—all through the Twenties and early Thirties—he continued campaigning for his endowment fund to be officially embraced by Rotary International. Yet his idea was met with responses ranging from indifference by some to an active underground effort to scuttle the fund from some senior Rotary leaders of the day. You see, some people are satisfied by the *status quo* and are resistant to change, whereas others recognize that we are always in changing times and need to open our eyes to new opportunities for service.

"But despite the behind-the-scenes politicking against his idea, Arch Klumph never gave up; never took his eyes off the prize.

"Six years after that first gift in 1918, the total in the fund was only $5,000. It was not until Paul Harris's death in 1947—and the Founder's specific instructions that no statues or memorials should be built—that the Rotary International board created the opportunity for gifts to be sent to what we now call The Rotary Foundation in Paul's name, for the purpose of fostering 'understanding and friendly relations between peoples of different nations.' Even in 1954, six years after Rotary International's big push for The Rotary Foundation, total annual giving only reached $500,000. It was not until 1965 that donations exceeded one million dollars for the first time in a single year. That was less than a half-century ago, and in 2006, The Rotary Foundation named the one-millionth Paul Harris Fellow. Imagine that! One million people have now donated $1,000 or more to the Foundation that Arch Klumph envisioned as being able to 'do good in the world.'

"Family of Rotary, this is a man who had almost no chance to succeed in life. He had neither the wealth, nor education, nor opportunity, nor family background to give him any hope of significance in the world. However, he did have vision, persistence, and a single-minded drive to make his dreams come true. In his second year as a Rotarian, he described himself as a man who 'thinks Rotary, sleeps Rotary, and dreams Rotary.'

"Now, let us think in present tense. The needs in our world are just as profound today, and I would argue, thanks to television, the Internet, and instant global communications, we are more *aware* of those needs than ever before.

"I don't know most of you, but I also feel comfortable in reaching this conclusion without fear of contradiction: many people in this room have more wealth, more education, a better background, and more resources than did Arch Klumph.

"So here's my question: if a man like Arch Klumph could make such a positive impact on humankind that seventy-five years later hundreds of thousands of people are alive and in decent housing; disease-free, living lives of dignity with productive jobs—think what effect *you* could have.

"Arch Klumph ended up owning several very successful companies: can we use the excuse 'I don't have time' with any degree of validity?

"Arch Klumph had to fight tooth and nail those naysayers who did not even think Rotary could, or should, support international humanitarian service.

However, for us, the infrastructure is already in place. We do not have to create anything. We simply have to add fuel to the well-oiled machine that runs night and day and that we know as The Rotary Foundation.

"You see, my friends, Arch Klumph left us the gift of The Rotary Foundation, but in truth, but he gave us much more: he left a legacy to humankind. It has been said that every person, no matter what gender, race, creed, or religion, no matter whether he is rich or poor, ultimately passes from this earth. When he does, a tombstone will be erected carrying his or her name. And right below that will be the date of birth, and then a dash, and then the date of his death.

"My fellow Rotarians, the most important part of that entire headstone is not the person's name, or touching tribute, or religious symbol. The most important thing is...*the dash.*

"What will *our* dash symbolize, ladies and gentlemen? Arch Klumph's dash led to the elimination of Polio around the world, to the advancing of peace and understanding between people, to a mighty flame of volunteerism that will never be extinguished.

"What will *your* dash represent?"

I paused to show them that this was not merely a hypothetical question. "Don't let me intimidate you," I continued. "You don't have to start a movement as great as The Rotary Foundation. Nevertheless, you can still leave a legacy. Why not lead a Group Study Exchange team to another country? On the other hand, if you do not have enough time for that, host an incoming GSE team in your club? Why not take a small percentage of every paycheck you get—whether it is a salary, or a big commission, or a small Social Security check, and put it into a savings account designated for The Rotary Foundation? Why not get together with a few friends and agree to become PolioPlus Partners—underwriting the cost of a specific need for a National Immunization Day? Why not make a trip that will live with you forever? A volunteer work mission to a Rotary Foundation-sponsored project?

"Or think about this: what if you were to endow a Rotary Peace Scholarship? That student, imbued with the skills taught at Rotary Peace Centers at one of the world's top universities could end up as an ambassador, foreign affairs minister, or national leader—and could use those peacemaking skills to avoid a future war, or help reconcile others already in conflict. What a legacy *you* could leave!

> "Endeavor to live so that when you die, even the undertaker will be sorry."
> – Mark Twain

"Am I dreaming dreams too large?

"Arch Klumph once said, 'there is no limit to the opportunities for Rotary to spread its field of service.' In 1928, when Rotary International officially created the endowment fund as a distinct entity and renamed it The Rotary Foundation, Klumph reminded Rotarians that the Foundation would be the key to Rotary's future. He said, 'We should look at the Foundation as being something not of today or tomorrow, but think of it in terms of the years and generations to come. Rotary is a movement for the centuries.'

"My Rotary friends, it matters little what you did yesterday: the future begins today. Of course, it is important to bring new members into Rotary. Obviously, we should be active in our clubs and work hard to provide service and fellowship through all Four Avenues of Service.

"But if you want to leave a legacy that will live long after you've passed on, if you want your life to have stood for something significant, then today—this weekend—is the new beginning. The future begins now. The decisions and commitment *you* make at this conference could lead one hundred years from now to a speaker describing you as the Rotarian who led....."

I paused again, and then continued slowly, enunciating each syllable:

"One

"Extraordinary

"Life."

"Rotarians are the heart and soul of Rotary. But our Rotary Foundation is its backbone. The Foundation is what makes so much of our great work possible. The Matching Grants, humanitarian grants, 3-H grants, Ambassadorial Scholarships, Group Study Exchanges, Rotary Peace Centers, and the major funding for PolioPlus are all possible through our Rotary Foundation funds.

Rotarians come to Rotary because they want to help make this world a better place. Well, The Rotary Foundation is what helps us do it.

Many Rotarians do not understand that The Rotary Foundation is a separate entity from Rotary. It has its own staff, its own finances, and its own administrative structure. It also receives all of its income separately from Rotary International. That is something that you need to make sure that all Rotarians in your district understand. Their membership dues do not go to our Foundation; only their donations go to our Foundation. That is why it is so important to tell Rotarians about our Foundation's Every Rotarian, Every Year effort. The Every Rotarian, Every Year initiative is the way we're going to ensure the long-term health of Rotary and the viability of all the wonderful work that Rotarians do."

– Frank Devlyn, Chairman,
The Rotary Foundation Trustees, 2005-2006

## CHAPTER 3

# TRF.101

**"G**ood morning fellow Rotarians, ladies and gentlemen, and welcome to the first plenary session of this very first regional Rotary Foundation conference."

It was Sue, as conference chair, who was now at the lectern. Following my opening keynote address, the delegates had taken a short refreshment break and they now reconvened for the "meat" of the conference. At Sue's invitation, I had sat in on a breakfast meeting she had held that morning with her conference planning team, which included the Rotary Foundation chairs from each of the four districts that had organized the conference. Three of the four district governors, and several other Rotary leaders—including the past-Regional Rotary Foundation Coordinator—had also attended the "Kick-off Breakfast."

I was impressed by how well planned the event appeared, and at how clear its objectives seemed to be to the organizers. They identified their goals to be:

1) To make Rotarians feel proud of the work of The Rotary Foundation

2) To make them more knowledgeable of The Rotary Foundation

3) To give them a sense of ownership in The Rotary Foundation

4) To motivate Rotarians to want to either become volunteers, or advocates for voluntary service to people they know.

5) To increase their personal financial support for The Rotary Foundation, and on a continuing basis—and to become advocates for Rotary Foundation donations from people they know.

The applause subsided and Sue continued, her face shown on a large screen to the right of the podium.

"Three years ago, I decided to make The Rotary Foundation a central focus of my year as club president. But I have a confession to make: I found it so confusing that I almost gave up on the idea before my year began."

I heard a few "Uh-huhs" near me and saw several heads nodding in agreement.

"I mean, it's a good thing to have *so many* programs and projects and giving opportunities ... but when you're new to all this and you are trying to understand it all, it's a *bad* thing to have *so many* programs and projects and giving opportunities!"

I saw more heads nodding and several people laughing.

"So I went to school on The Rotary Foundation, and realized that until *I* could understand it, I couldn't sell it to my club. Moreover, until I could sell it to the club, I could never expect a successful outcome. My fellow Rotarians, support of our Foundation is too important for us to fail."

There was a ripple of applause.

"It was inspiring to hear Frank Devlyn tell us about the origins of The Rotary Foundation a little while ago, and after learning about the extraordinary life that Arch Klumph led, I certainly feel both an *obligation* to do more, and somewhat overwhelmed at what big shoes I, as one ordinary Rotarian, have to fill. However, while we should all be proud of the wonderful history our Foundation has, in truth, I suspected that history alone would not motivate many of my club members to become involved today. They asked me to tell you how I made my own club more informed on The Rotary Foundation, so let us begin.

"First, I formed a committee and we met for several weeks in advance of my induction as club president. They were charged with learning as much as possible about The Rotary Foundation and then delivering a 'Rotary Foundation Moment' each week at our club meeting. They also wrote short articles for each weekly club bulletin. We broke the information down into two broad categories—much as we have done for this plenary session. First, there were The Rotary Foundation's programs. That was the 'What do they do?' part. Second, we communicated the financial giving opportunities. We called that the 'How you can make dreams come true?' part.

"So let's start with an overview of the programs. As you will see from the handout you all received, this is very much a general 'big picture' presentation. It would take days to go in-depth into every Rotary Foundation program. We wanted to give our members a perspective of just how many lives their Rotary Foundation touches. We grouped the programs into three categories: educational, humanitarian, and PolioPlus. Let us look at these together.

"The Rotary Foundation *began* with educational programs, and today, tens of thousands of former

Rotary Foundation scholars are dotted around the world—often occupying the highest offices in business and government. The best-known program is Ambassadorial Scholarships, whose goal is to provide scholarships for degree-level study abroad. There are special set-asides for cultural scholarships and for students from low-income countries. It costs The Rotary Foundation around $25,000 for a one-year Ambassadorial scholarship. Past students say the term is well chosen, since during their year abroad they live and interact with people in a foreign country and feel like ambassadors for their homeland. Yet after learning so much about another culture, when they return, they can speak of the people in that foreign land with the knowledge and closeness of an ambassador.

"The Rotary Foundation also has grants of up to $22,500 for university teachers who agree to teach at colleges in low-income countries. This wonderful program builds understanding and development between wealthy and third-world nations while providing further education to the next generation in poor countries.

> "The message is not 'Get a 4.0 and hole up in your room studying.' It is 'Go out there, build bridges, learn, and connect the world.' I love that."
> –Ruby Powers, Ambassadorial Scholar from San Antonio, Texas who studied in Barcelona, Spain.

"The program most familiar to Rotarians in this room today is GSE—Group Study Exchange. Every year, each of the 530 Rotary districts around the world selects four non-Rotarians aged 25-40, along with a Rotarian team leader. The district is then matched with a district in another country, and for four-to-six weeks, the team is hosted by that district. That same year, the receiving district sends its own GSE team to the sending district. Group Study Exchange enables outstanding young business and professional people to experience the culture, judicial and political systems, and true fellowship of people in a faraway land. Many of you have enjoyed memorable personal encounters with GSE team leaders. I know in my own district we took the GSE team from Zambia into our homes and learned things about Zambia that none of knew before. While they were with us, we matched up team members with people in our own club and community having similar vocations. I remember one was a journalist, and he spent a day at our newspaper offices seeing how it compared to his own paper. We had a surgeon, whom a member of my club arranged to join him in the O.R and another team member—an attorney—spent a day in court with a lawyer from my club. There was no question how this experience brought the two groups of people closer together. Someone said later, 'Before that GSE team came, I couldn't have even found Zambia on a map—let alone told you anything about it. Now, I find myself taking a real interest if that country is mentioned in the media.' This year, our district is sending a uni-vocational GSE team—where all the members are in different health-related fields—to Estonia. I know we will be doing our small part to sow seeds of friendship and cross-cultural understanding between our two countries. Lifelong friendships are often forged from when two people meet in a GSE exchange

"Finally, we end our section on The Rotary Foundation's educational programs by explaining the newest project: the Rotary Centers for International Studies in Peace and Conflict Resolution. Degreed individuals who wish to pursue a career in peacemaking may apply to The Rotary Foundation for this unique graduate-level program. Each year, 70 of them receive a full scholarship to earn a master's degree in peace and conflict resolution at one of the Rotary Centers for International Studies at seven leading universities around the world. All their travel, tuition, room, and board are included. There is even a new short-term Rotary Peace and Conflict Studies Fellowship Program that I am sure the world will accept enthusiastically. It was the brainchild of Past Rotary International President Bhichai Rattakul.

"So to summarize, the Foundation's *educational* programs—which are always adapting to changing times—include Ambassadorial Scholarships for undergraduates, grants for university teachers to work in colleges in underdeveloped countries, Group Study Exchange, and the exciting new Rotary Peace Scholarships. Now let's move on to The Rotary Foundation's humanitarian programs."

Sue took a large sip of water, looked at the screen to be sure the correct slide was showing, and began again.

"One of our most beloved humanitarian endeavors is the one we all call *Three H*: Health, Hunger, and Humanity. Their purpose is to find long-term—meaning two-to-four-year—international development projects to improve health, alleviate hunger, and enhance development through sustainable self-help activities. These are not Band-Aid projects. They must be initiated and implemented by Rotarians, be self-sustaining once grant funding has ended, and must benefit a larger number of people. The Rotary Foundation typically provides $100,000 to $300,000 for each 3H grant.

"But what if Rotarians identify a compelling need that does not meet the substantial qualifying criteria for 3H? The Rotary Foundation funds hundreds of smaller projects through its Matching Grants program. Rotarians in two or more countries agree to sponsor a humanitarian project, and after they raise some of the necessary money themselves, they apply to The Rotary Foundation for a matching grant for the balance.

"Not long after I joined Rotary, I remember hearing one member of my club complain that he would not contribute to The Rotary Foundation because all the money went overseas, and he felt some should stay in our local community. I thought his views were rather selfish—especially for a member of an *international* service organization, but they were his, nonetheless. Well today, he has no basis for his complaint, because The Rotary Foundation makes available money for local humanitarian service projects right in our home area through its District Simplified Grants. I know of one district that suffered terrible floods—and The Rotary Foundation gave them more than $20,000 to

The effect of the Group Study Exchange between District 4930 Argentina and District 6950 Florida has lasted long past their 2003-2004 trip. Illustrating Rotary's goal of international understanding and friendship, the exchange has led to the development of several long-term projects, including the creation of a pen pal program between children in the two countries.

The exchange of letters, organized by one of the GSE team members who is an ESOL teacher in Argentina, has been especially eye opening for the children from Argentina, whose limited means have kept them from meeting people even in neighboring towns. Plans are now in the works for Rotarians in Florida to provide the Argentinean children with the school supplies they need.

provide relief to the victims. Another club received a District Simplified Grant to build a playground and park."

Sue took another sip of water.

"That brings me to the last section: PolioPlus. Although I have heard some Rotarians grumble that Rotary has not received enough media recognition for our PolioPlus Campaign, the fact remains that we are not doing it for the publicity—we are in this campaign for the millions of lives we have already saved through this one, incredible, amazing program. Bob will tell us of his own hands-on experience with PolioPlus later this afternoon, but let me give you an overview of PolioPlus within the context of The Rotary Foundation's programs. The goal, quite simply, is to eradicate polio—globally. Working with our partners the World Health Organization, Centers for Disease Control, and UNICEF, we have already reduced the number of new polio cases by ninety-nine percent since PolioPlus began in 1988. Our Rotary Foundation has spent hundreds of millions of your contributions to immunize children in 122 countries, and then to monitor mop-up and follow-through activities so that when the country goes three years without any new cases, the World Health Organization can certify it polio free.

"Some of you may have also heard of PolioPlus Partners. This is where individuals, clubs, or districts can contribute through The Rotary Foundation to *support* the polio eradication campaigns. For example, other than the cost of the actual vaccine, money is needed for tents, uniforms to identify the volunteers, signs, cold storage boxes, printed posters and billboards, and so on. These support activities that make a national immunization day possible are funded by PolioPlus Partners grants.

"Well, my fellow Rotarians, that is an overview of the programs of The Rotary Foundation so how does the Foundation—*our* Foundation—get the money to fund these incredible projects? Yes, from you and from me! Surely, only the most self-centered person would decide *not* to contribute to our Foundation. For the rest of us..."

She paused for effect, drawing several chuckles from the large audience.

"For the rest of us, the question is, *how* can we give to The Rotary Foundation—and how should we designate our gift? This was also part of the weekly Rotary Foundation Moment we shared with my club members the year I was president.

"We begin with the Annual Programs Fund—the core of all the Foundation's program support. Contributions that we send to the Annual Programs Fund are invested by the Foundation for three years, after which fifty percent of the original donation is used to fund the humanitarian and GSE programs I described earlier. So what happens to the other fifty percent? It is returned to our district three years later in a credit called District Designated Funds—or DDF. Our district then decides how these funds are spent. Perhaps for a PolioPlus Partners grant, or to sponsor an Ambassadorial scholar, or for a Matching Grant.

"The other way we can designate our contributions to The Rotary Foundation is to the Permanent Fund. This ensures the long-term viability of our Foundation and its programs. Every penny we designate to the Permanent Fund *stays* in the Permanent Fund. However, it is an endowment, and Rotary's expert financial managers invest this money. Moreover, while the core funds are never used, the income they generate is used to expand existing programs and underwrite new ones—all within the criteria established by the Foundation for humanitarian, educational, and cultural assistance. As you can imagine, the larger the core Permanent Fund grows, the more income it generates—and the more programs The Rotary Foundation can provide in the future, without having to rely on new fundraising campaigns to Rotarians.

"When we move into the next session, which we call The Rotary Foundation Marketplace, you will find a table with knowledgeable folks who can give you literature and answer any questions you may have about how to contribute to your Foundation—including a booklet on how to include The Rotary Foundation in your will.

"My friends and fellow Rotarians, I learned as club president that one cardinal sin was to overrun the allotted time for a Rotary meeting. As chair of today's event, I know I have only four minutes left in my slot—so let me finish with a personal thought that should take only half that long. Compared to many of you, I am the new kid on the block. I joined Rotary because this man ..."

She pointed at me.

"... sat next to me on a train when we all had a cancelled flight. For the first year or so, I liked Rotary well enough, but it became, quite honestly, rather humdrum for me. When my club elected me president, I agreed—without inner enthusiasm—out of a sense of duty. But then I discovered the *real* secret of Rotary: the joy that comes from serving others—and how we can do that through The Rotary Foundation.

"Friends, it changed my life. My dear friend Bob, who will speak to us this afternoon, entranced me with his story of immunizing babies against polio. Another friend, Duncan, showed me the difference between giving a nod to humanitarian service—and enthusiastically embracing it. You will hear from Duncan, too. I do not know how much longer I will be on this earth—few of us do. However, this I can tell you with certainty: I want my life to have meant something. I want it to have had *significance*. Acting alone, how much can I do? However, The Rotary Foundation gives me the vehicle to make an impact. I can volunteer today, I can support others who do so tomorrow, and I can designate some of the financial gifts with which I have been blessed so that long, long after I have passed from this earth, I will still be enabling The Rotary Foundation to be saving lives, eliminating suffering, and promoting peace.

"How about you, my family of Rotary? How about you?"

As Sue left the podium, the audience erupted into sustained applause. She had, I thought, taken a complex subject and made it relevant and understandable to every person in the room. She was indeed an eloquent spokesperson for our Foundation!

Astrid Wenkel was a 2001-2002 Ambassadorial Scholar sponsored by District 1800 in Germany to study in District 9940 in New Zealand. In addition to her studies, Astrid used her time in New Zealand to raise awareness of the plight of "The Children of Pavlovsk." As part of her Master's degree program in Germany, Astrid had to do six months of practical training. She spent those six months with the non-governmental organization, working as a peace volunteer in a state-run orphanage for handicapped children in Russia. The Russian state was unable to provide funds to properly care for orphans with physical or mental disabilities. These children could not walk or play, nor did they have proper nutrition and supplies.

Since her time in Russia, Astrid has worked tirelessly to raise funds to purchase necessities for these forgotten children and her scholarship year was no different. With the help of host Rotarians, Astrid helped make these kids one of District 9940's Humanitarian Projects after she presented information about them to Rotary clubs throughout the South Pacific region. She led the Rotarians of District 9940 in raising NZ $13,200 for the orphanage, which will supply 150 handicapped orphans with food and other essential items. Astrid's achievements are certainly impressive and touching, and are great examples of how the Ambassadorial Scholarship can be used to foster international understanding and world peace.

CHAPTER 4

# At the Marketplace

As the applause from Sue's speech subsided, the sergeant at arms asked conference delegates to move to the adjacent ballroom. The next session, he explained, would be an open forum. The committee had arranged tables throughout the meeting room, each with a large sign denoting the topic of discussion that they would hold at that spot. "So if you are interested in Group Study Exchange, go to the GSE table. If you need to know how to sponsor an Ambassadorial scholar, or apply for a matching grant, look for those signs and go to the appropriate table. Be sure to also stop by the table under the signs 'Rotary Action Groups' and 'Rotary Fellowships.'

"This is a new idea in Rotary where Rotarians who share a common vocation or interest can channel their energies and enthusiasm into one specific area," the sergeant at arms continued. "This could be a resource group for some Rotary Foundation activities. For example, I am very involved in an orphanage I helped start in Botswana, that cares for children whose parents died from AIDS. We have a Rotary Action Group for Rotarians Fighting AIDS, so this allows me to work with other Rotarians having a similar interest and we can leverage our efforts and perhaps cooperate on common grant submissions."

He explained the next session would last one hour, and be divided into four 15-minute segments, thus allowing attendees to gain knowledge and insight in four different aspects of The Rotary Foundation. A Rotarian experienced in the topic of his or her table would remain there for all four sessions to facilitate discussions and answer questions, but everybody else would then rotate to another table when the bell rang every 15 minutes. I learned that I was free to circulate wherever I wanted as the "Roving Rotary Foundation Ambassador."

"Oh, I almost forgot!" he added. "That session begins at exactly eleven o'clock, so you have 12 minutes to use the rest rooms and help yourselves to refreshments, both of which you will find in the hallway over there to my right."

As I leaned over to retrieve my notebook, I heard a man's voice. "Frank! I am so sorry I did not get to greet you earlier. How are you?" I turned and saw Bob approaching me with outstretched arms and just behind him was Duncan.

"Bob! Duncan! *Hola, amigos.* I am very well; how are you? My word, you haven't changed a bit since I first met you guys on the train that morning what, six years ago now?"

"Well, that's not entirely true," Bob corrected me with a rueful smile. I put on a bit here." He pointed to his waist.

"And I've lost a bit more up here." Duncan pointed to his hair.

We all laughed.

"Guys, I have to tell you, I am absolutely thrilled to be here. What a difference I feel from the sense I had when I was last in your district. Sue and I had a long talk on the way in from the airport last night, and all three of you seem to be really motivated, excited Rotarians now. And this Rotary Foundation conference, so far, is the best I have ever seen."

"That's because of Sue," said Duncan. "She somehow caught the Rotary Foundation bug during her year as club president and has been a real dynamo ever since. People are *excited* to support the Foundation now."

"I could not agree more," Bob concurred. "You may remember, Frank, that I had all-but quit Rotary the last time we met. However, you persuaded me to give it another chance, and I am so glad I did. In retrospect, I believe I was rather selfish before. I was thinking, '*I'm* bored. Rotary is not doing anything for *me*. *I* don't have time for this.' It was all about *me*. By putting the focus on The Rotary Foundation in her presidential year, and seeing with my own eyes what a difference one person can make, I realized that real joy comes from serving others. It is not about *me*, it's all about *them*."

"That's quite a testament, Bob," I said, quite moved at how this young man had matured. When we first met, his life seemed to revolve around material things—his cars, money, his hi-tech toys—and on enjoying the good life. Apparently, marriage, promotion into management, twin baby daughters—and perhaps Rotary—had made him into a much more considerate, compassionate human being.

"But Frank, I am not in Sue and Bob's club," said Duncan. "And the same change has begun to occur all over our district. Even during the year she was club president, word leaked out that amazing things were happening there. I often chose to make up meetings at Bob's club—even when I did not need a makeup! The district governor was very wise to ask Sue to serve as district Rotary Foundation chair, because she certainly has changed the paradigm for all of us."

"In what way?" I asked.

"Well, I don't want to criticize anybody in particular," Duncan answered, glancing around as if to be sure he would not be overheard. "But in the past, it was the same old people bringing the same old message. There was never an invitation for hands-on involvement, where we could actually *see* what The Rotary Foundation does. It was always about money."

"He's right," Bob affirmed. "If you saw the district Rotary Foundation chairman at a club meeting, you knew what his speech was going to be:

'Fellow Rotarians, this is Rotary Foundation month. Please give $1,000 to make someone a Paul Harris Fellow. It is tax deductible.' Or,

'The district conference is coming up next month and the governor is short on his Rotary Foundation goal this year. Why not make yourself a Paul Harris Fellow and have the Rotary International President's Representative present it to you at the conference?' Gag me with a spoon!"

"Tell Frank about the two dollars, Bob," Duncan urged, with an impish smile.

"Oh, please! For an entire year, the governor at the time and his Rotary Foundation chairman had two-dollar bills stapled to their jacket lapels. Every freaking event they attended, there was that stupid two-dollar bill. Finally, in maybe June—almost at the end of his term in office—someone in my club came right out and asked him, 'Hey, governor! What's with the two-dollar bill?' It was almost as if he had forgotten it was there—and that he had been walking around with it stapled to the front of his jacket for the past 365 days. 'That,' he said, proudly, 'is to remind every Rotarian that if they give two dollars a week to The Rotary Foundation, it will add up to one hundred dollars a year. Our new theme is *Every Rotarian Every Year.*'

"I thought the guy at my table was going to have a heart attack. 'That's the dumbest thing I've ever seen!' he said to the governor. 'First of all, you've been governor for eleven months and only now do the rank-and-file Rotarians understand what you want us to do. Second, if wearing a two-dollar bill on your jacket symbolizes that we should give to The Rotary Foundation, why not wear soup on your tie to remind people to support the food bank?' That got a lot of laughs."

"Well, Bob, I have to defend the guy," I said. "One of the problems we have encountered at The Rotary Foundation is that many people have contributed $1,000 to make themselves a Paul Harris Fellow, and then they never give again. They think they have already taken care of The Rotary Foundation forever. Moreover, unbelievably, thirty percent of Rotary clubs give nothing

> "The Rotary Foundation is not to build monuments of brick and stone. If we work upon marble, it will perish; if we work on brass, time will efface it; if we rear temples they will crumble into dust; but if we work upon immortal minds, if we imbue them with the full meaning of the spirit of Rotary... we are engraving on those tablets something that will brighten all eternity."
> – Arch C. Klumph, Founder, The Rotary Foundation

to The Rotary Foundation and only thirty percent of Rotarians personally give anything to the Foundation. The *Every Rotarian Every Year* campaign is to raise awareness that they should include The Rotary Foundation in their benevolence budget on an ongoing basis."

"I don't have a problem with the campaign, Frank." Bob argued. "I have a problem with how poorly it was communicated. Of all the people I know in Rotary, not one person every said, 'Gee, look at that fellow walking around with a two-dollar bill stapled to his jacket. I really feel compelled to donate to The Rotary Foundation now.'"

"I have a different objection to the method that PDG chose," Duncan interjected. Yes, I agree with Bob that the communication was not handled well. However, my argument is this: who is Rotary, or that district governor, to decide that $100 a year is the amount I should give? I am sure he would argue that the $100 is an *average* amount between Rotarians around the world, and that to some, $100 is a lot of money. But by suggesting a specific amount, they are limiting the possibilities, in my opinion."

"Well, I don't think he was limiting the amount to one hundred dollars," I explained. "I suspect he chose that as an example."

"But that was not his message, Frank." Duncan continued. "Every time I heard him speak that year, every mention of the *Every Rotarian Every Year* campaign in the governor's newsletter cited the example of how giving two dollars a week amounted to *one hundred dollars a year*, as if that was an incredible feat. My point is we have missed all those people who have the ability to far exceed that amount. And that is the area I am handling as a member of Sue's Rotary Foundation committee this year."

"Tell more," I asked him.

"Sue says that our first goal is to educate and motivate. We need to tell people about the amazing work The Rotary Foundation is doing, and motivate or inspire them to take ownership in it—to really feel as if it is *their* foundation. My role on the committee is to raise Rotary Foundation contributions by twenty-five percent or more over last year's total."

"Twenty-five percent! That is incredible. How do you propose doing that, Duncan?" I asked.

"Once we have educated and motivated them— and this conference is an example of how we are doing that—we are using the Three P's approach to the members. In contrast to the campaign Bob and I just told you about, where everyone was expected to give the same two dollars a week, we are asking Rotarians to make their gifts personal, proportionate to their wealth, and to pledge on an annual basis. You will hear more about that when I give my presentation this afternoon. If I tell you now, you might fall asleep during my talk!"

"I very much doubt that, Duncan." I assured him, slapping him on his back. He was an amazing man. I guessed he must be in his mid-seventies, yet he had the energy and enthusiasm of someone half his age.

"Speaking of falling asleep, I need a cup of coffee," said Bob. "Why don't we move into the hallway, grab a coffee, and then see what's going on in the Rotary Foundation Marketplace. They are about to begin, and I don't want to get the blame for making the guest of honor late." We all agreed and worked our way through the crowd surrounding the refreshment stations in the hallway.

I was very impressed when I entered the next ballroom. There must have been 20 tables around the room, each sporting a large sign. I could see *PolioPlus Partners, GSE, Volunteer Trips, Planned Giving, Peace Scholars,* and *Fundraising Ideas* above the row of tables closest to me. Most tables already had a throng of people around them when the bell rang to signal the start of the first session.

As I walked over to the *Ambassadorial Scholars* table, one Rotarian was asking the facilitator what affect the program had once the scholar completed his or her studies and returned home. "Do Rotary Foundation Ambassadorial Scholars ever amount to anything, or are we spending a lot of our money sending them on a free year-long trip abroad that never results in them actually contributing much to society?"

All eyes turned to the facilitator, a middle-aged woman in a dark blue suit wearing the nametag "Nancy."

"I think that is a fair question," she answered. "After all, we are asking you to be proud of this program and to support it with your donations. You have every right to know how effective the program has been. Since the first Ambassadorial Scholarship was awarded back in 1948, thirty-six thousand students from 110 nations have benefited from the program. One rose to become prime minister of Portugal, one became Britain's Governor to Australia; one was later U.S. Ambassador to Great Britain. Van Cliburn, who won the renowned Tchaikovsky International Piano Competition, was a Rotary Foundation Ambassadorial Scholar. So was Steve Downing, who now oversees the entire $65-million budget for CARE in India. Paul Volker, former chairman of the Federal Reserve Bank was an Ambassadorial Scholar—oh, and so was Sadako Ogata, who went on to become the United Nations High Commissioner for Refugees. In fact, The Rotary Foundation's Ambassadorial Scholarship program is now the largest privately funded university program in the world.

"I made some copies of this, in case you are interested," said Nancy. This was an article in *The Rotarian* magazine a while back about a teacher in Estonia who dreamed of learning the latest teaching methods from the United States. She successfully applied for one of the 35 Ambassadorial Scholarships each year that are reserved for students from low-income countries. As a result, she earned her degree at Loyola University in Chicago and when she returned to Estonia was able to make an enormous difference in the lives of the children she taught, especially those with disabilities."

Nancy reached into a file folder and removed another single piece of paper, which she passed around.

"And this is one of my favorite testimonials of the Ambassadorial Scholarship program. It is from Bill Moyers, the renowned Public Television news anchor. Before he went into broadcasting, he joined the Peace Corps, ultimately becoming its deputy director. Look at what he said of his experience as a Rotary Foundation scholar: 'What we do is touch other people ... open the horizon to them ... and tell them: *you matter.* You see, the five men who chose me to become a Rotary Ambassadorial Scholar are gone ... but they are not. They never will be. Because along the way, I will in my own way share with others—and have—what those five men and the 60 members of the Marshall (Texas) Rotary Club, and the tens of thousands of other members of Rotary did in 1956 when they said, *Bill Moyers, you can matter.*' What a message our scholarship alumni can send to the world."

"I'm sold!" The man who had asked the question threw up his hands in mock surrender. "I can hardly believe it. I have been in Rotary for seven years and had no idea we had this sort of project. I am a teacher; so obviously, I am a strong believer in education. How can I become more involved in the Ambassadorial Scholarships program in my own club?"

Nancy referred to a clipboard and gave the man the name of his district's Ambassadorial Scholarship Program chair, suggesting that he call him and volunteer to serve on the committee, or at least to meet so he could have all his questions answered.

"I see President Frank Devlyn is with us," she added. "Frank, is there anything you would like to share on the subject?"

"Nancy, I think you're doing a great job all by yourself," I said. "This is *your* discussion group. I don't want to take it over." Then a thought suddenly came to me. "There is one thing that I just remembered," I added.

"Some of you may have heard of Hogie Hansen. Hogie is a great guy; a past district governor who retired early and came to Rotary headquarters for a couple of years to volunteer in a senior capacity on The Rotary Foundation. Well, Hogie told me the story of how he had once had a teacher by the name of Robert Dunn, who had been a Rotary Foundation Ambassadorial Scholar. He left a lasting impact on Hogie's life, and over the years, Hogie kept in close contact with Mr. Dunn and his wife. As they became more financially comfortable, and as they learned more about our Foundation from Hogie, they decided to pass on the blessing of a scholarship to worthy individuals by endowing a permanent Ambassadorial Scholarship with The Rotary Foundation."

"That's exactly what your speech was about this morning," a man at the far end of the table interjected.

"What was?" I asked.

"Leaving a legacy." He explained. "That teacher has now left a legacy. The Rotary Foundation scholarship they endowed will be part of their 'dash.'"

"Well now I know at least one person was listening!" I said. "Folks, this is one of the brightest jewels in Rotary's crown. I'm going to check out some other tables and leave you to let Nancy inspire you about the Ambassadorial Scholarship program." Several people raised their hand to wave and I wandered over to the group beneath a *Matching Grants* sign.

"But there is so much corruption in many developing countries. How can we be sure our money is spent the way we intended?" A tall, rather sophisticated woman was quizzing the facilitator about a project I assumed she was interested in starting.

"You have just touched on one of the great strengths of Rotary Foundation Matching Grants," the table host answered. "We insist on total accountability. That is why you must work in partnership with a Rotary club or district in the local community. Rotarians are responsible for ensuring only legitimate expenses are paid, and they must in turn receive approval from their district governor and district Foundation chair. We are not a bank. Rotarians are our eyes and ears on the ground and they must be involved in every aspect of the project, including financial accountability and the work on the project itself. The Rotary Foundation will not release one dime of the grant money until all the accounting safeguards have been submitted and verified. Here are the forms that explain the strict qualification criteria, and I want to warn you, every application is carefully scrutinized on both a district level and at The Rotary Foundation office by the Matching Grants subcommittee."

I thought of a Matching Grant application I had been involved in a few years earlier when Rotarians from New Jersey, USA had worked with a district in Recife, Brazil to buy and operate a mobile eye clinic. The vehicle traveled into some of the continent's most impoverished communities, providing first-rate care ranging from eyeglasses to cataract and refractive surgery. A year later, I had received a letter from a woman whose sight had been restored by ophthalmologists in the Rotary mobile eye clinic. "Thank you for giving me my sight." She had written. "But most of all, thank you for giving me the most precious gift of now being able to see my baby daughter for the first time." *Yes, I thought, you do not have to convince me of the value of a Rotary Foundation Matching Grant.* I had since gone on to help form the Avoidable Blindness Donor Advised Fund for people who wanted their gifts to The Rotary Foundation to specifically help with projects such as the one in Recife, and we now have eye clinics all over the world—typically restoring sight to cataract victims for as little as $33 in India. That's quite a difference considering the same procedure costs about $2,000 in the USA.

"Mr. Devlyn?" I turned to see a young man with a bright red beard standing behind me, a notebook in his right hand.

"Yes."

"My name is Pete Murphy. I am a reporter with the *Times-Herald*, the largest newspaper in town. I am doing a story on this conference and they suggested I ask you a couple of questions. Do you have a minute?"

"Of course," I replied.

"I have spent quite a while walking around in here, so I feel I have a good idea what sort of activities The Rotary Foundation conducts. But tell me, Mr. Devlyn, what are the corporate goals of The Rotary Foundation?"

"The mission of The Rotary Foundation is to build world understanding and peace through international humanitarian and educational programs," I said, hoping I had remembered the mission statement accurately. I had recently chaired the Future Vision Committee, which was planning to introduce an updated version of the Foundation's mission—one that kept pace with our changing times, but I did not want to confuse the issue here.

"Well, that sounds impressive," the reporter said. "But it also sounds like just another platitude. Like, 'I wish we had world peace and no more hunger and that the whole world could just live in harmony.'"

I sensed he was challenging me. "First of all, what is wrong with such a goal?" I asked him. "Would you argue for the alternative? Do you think world war, hunger, and universal animosity and suffering is better?"

"Of course not," he said. "My point was that there is probably not a person in this country who would not want...what did you call it...world understanding and peace, but what can we do about it? We are just individuals. The governments make wars and peace, not the people."

"And who elects the governments?" I asked. "What I believe is that there is of course a need for governments and national policies. However, there is also a need for action on the grass-roots level. Margaret Mead once said, 'Never doubt that a small group of thoughtful, committed citizens can change the world. Indeed, it is the only thing that ever has.' Can I, Frank Devlyn, stop a war? No, of course not. Can you, Pete Murphy wipe out a disease? Of course not. But what if I work together with 1.2 million other people who all share my commitment to peace? And what if we then work together across the lines of the 170 countries we all come from, reaching out to appreciate that while we speak different languages and have different religions, we are all in need of prosperity, decent environments in which to raise our families, and the prospect of doing so without scourges such as diseases that could ruin our lives? Don't you think we could all agree on those basic needs?"

"I suppose so."

"So we *can* agree on some common values and aspirations. Now that group of people—the 1.2 million I just spoke of are called *Rotarians*—can work together not as a government or an army, but as a mighty, and influential, force that can help change people's attitudes and bring about change."

"But how would you describe The Rotary Foundation's work in terms of its relevance to ordinary people?" he asked.

I considered his question for a moment before responding. "Rotarians *care*." I began. "And caring means finding ways to say 'yes' when there are lots of ways to say 'no.'"

"Would you expand on that thought, please?"

"Sure. Rotarians are as difficult to narrowly define as any group of 1.2 million people in 170 countries would be. But while they are of different genders, ethnic heritage, ages, and vocations, they share a few similar values: they are strongly committed to ethical conduct, to service to their local communities, to promoting peace and goodwill between nations, and to helping people in need all over the world. Generally, Rotarians are business and professional leaders in their communities, yet they believe the best things in life are not *things*. Our members support The Rotary Foundation in two essential ways: they make financial donations to enable it to make grants, and they volunteer themselves to do hands-on work in projects all over the world. Time after time, when a Rotarian visits a site where The Rotary Foundation's work is being conducted, he or she sees with his own eyes how valuable our Foundation is, and they return home with renewed enthusiasm and determination to help that work continue. I remember one Rotarian from Canada who told me she had visited a site in Africa where The Rotary Foundation was working to eliminate river blindness. She told me she had never even thought of river blindness before, but that she had now returned home and become an advocate with local groups in her community to raise money and organize volunteer work teams to go back and help.

"I think it was Jackie Robinson who said, 'A life is not important except in the impact it has on other lives.' That describes what Rotarians do through The Rotary Foundation. They care for a bunch of forgotten people whom you will never interview; who will never make the evening news. To most folks, those starving in Ethiopia or without safe, clean drinking water in India or those without adequate neonatal care in Papua-New Guinea—to most people, they are, at best, faceless, nameless statistics. However, to Rotarians they are *real* people with *real* needs and we have a *real* mechanism for giving them a chance at life. That mechanism is The Rotary Foundation."

"Can you give me specific examples of your members who have done something tangible to address these needs you speak of?" he asked.

"My goodness, yes! How much time do you have?" I asked, rhetorically. "One Rotarian, John Hollyman, has maintained perfect attendance at Rotary meetings for fifty years. To commemorate this accomplishment, he and his wife Lyn donated over US$1 million in stocks to the Foundation's Permanent Fund, requesting that the spendable earnings from their gift be directed by the Trustees. I can think of several Japanese Rotarians—who have witnessed the horrors of war first hand—who have endowed Rotary World Peace Fellowships. Other Rotarians in Korea and Southeast Asia have made significant gifts to The Rotary Foundation that were used for avoidable blindness and other humanitarian efforts across Asia and into Africa. I have a friend who is a real estate broker in New Jersey. He saw the terrible plight of orphaned children in Romania. Now, you may ask, what can a New Jersey Realtor do about Romanian orphans? Not much, by himself. However, by harnessing the power of other caring, compassionate folks, he built his own orphanage, started a job-training program for street kids, opened a free clinic, and initiated the first early childhood education program in the country for children in the state orphanages. He could not have done that by himself, but by partnering with Rotarians in Romania, and in other countries who want to help Romanian orphans, one person *can* make a difference. The Rotary Foundation has provided a van to help transport the children between their orphanage and school.

"All of us: you, I, these people around us—have been given certain blessings in our lives. Moreover, all of us have an opportunity to share those with people who have not been so richly blessed. We can summarize our ability to give by what I call the Four T's: our thinking, our talent, our time, and our treasure. Some of our best minds become teachers because at one time a Rotary Foundation grant sent them to another country on an educational scholarship and they are now teaching tolerance, peace, and reconciliation. Others do not have a lot of money to give, but they can share their talents. Take you, for example, Pete. You are a journalist. Do you enjoy writing, or is it just a job for you?"

He looked at me quizzically, not sure whether I was taking a personal interest in him, or whether I had turned the tables and was now interviewing *him*. "No, I really love writing," he said. "I have done ever since I was in high school. For me, there is something wonderful in being able to take the written word and turn it into something persuasive, something poetic, something that brings both information and inspiration to the reader."

"That's great. That is your talent. Now imagine how you could use *your* talent to write an article on how people from right here in your hometown are performing selfless acts of humanitarian service that allow a woman to see her child for the first time. Or how you could volunteer to write a brochure or some press releases that spread the good news about the work the local Rotary clubs and The Rotary Foundation do to relieve suffering around the world. Can you see how you could help just by sharing your talents?"

"Yes," he answered. "I do."

"And although I don't know you and have never even met you before, I am guessing that just by doing that—let's say as a result of that article you wrote, three doctors volunteered to go on a Rotary volunteer trip and perform corrective surgery to landmine victims—I'll bet that would make you feel really good, wouldn't it?"

"It sure would."

"Now do you see my point? You are an ordinary person—not even a Rotarian, and yet by sharing you talent, you would have made a difference in the world to people whose names you do not know, but who need our help. Now imagine if you expanded your outreach to the other three T's and also went on a volunteer trip yourself. What if you shared your *time;* you spoke to your friends at the gym or at work and recruited them to the cause—you shared your *thinking,* and you took a small percentage of your income each payday and donated it to a needy cause—you shared your *treasure.* Now imagine how much more invested you would be in changing our world for the better."

"Mr. Devlyn, I have to tell you. I came here because I was given this assignment by my editor. I thought it would be a quick interview, in and out, kind of boring...but you have really made me think about the work these Rotarians are doing in the world. I think you have pricked my conscience. I can see that we really are all rather interconnected in what people call our global village. Good luck with the conference, and here is my card: by all

> The minutes of the September 18-20, 1917 meeting of Board of Directors of the International Association of Rotary Clubs (later to become Rotary International) contained the following observation from Rotary's founder, Paul Harris (then Counsel to the Association): "I have read the Section [proposing the establishment of an Endowment Fund] and see no legal objection to the Section."

means pass it along to the local Rotary club. I would be very interested in doing anything they might need me to do to share my talents. I want to thank you for your time." He gave me a firm handshake and looked me directly in the eye.

"I believe mankind is now on a new brink, not the brink of war, but the brink of peace ... Now is the time for our generation to build from the multitude of conflicting desires and persistent national and economic rivalries a new relationship among peoples, one that frees the energies among nations and their people for the constructive endeavors that will create a better life for all."

– W. Jack Davis, Hamilton, Bermuda.
President, Rotary International 1977-78.

## CHAPTER 5

# Let There Be Peace on Earth ...

It was lunchtime, and the delegates had just been given quite a shock: having taken their seats at elegantly accessorized tables in the large luxury hotel where the conference was being held, Sue had taken the podium. "My fellow Rotarians, a full-course luncheon was going to cost us thirty-five dollars today, by the time all the taxes and service charges had been included. So we have gone to 'Plan B.'"

She paused, sensing that she now had everybody's attention.

"We explained The Rotary Foundation's real purpose to the hotel management, and they agreed to let us have rolls and soup, with a green salad, for less than five dollars. We will serve ourselves and clear our own tables to cut the labor costs—and just from this simple gesture, we will today contribute the difference between our budgeted cost and the actual cost to our Rotary Foundation. Now I apologize if you were looking forward to a sumptuous lunch. But I looked at myself in the mirror as we walked down the hallway, and I don't think I really *need* this lunch..." she tapped her hips. "We estimate this one decision will amount to almost $21,000—all of which will be designated for hunger relief programs of The Rotary Foundation."

An enormous cheer erupted from around the dining room.

"But wait! It gets better: Governor Harriet spoke to President Frank a few minutes ago, and we will try to take that $21,000 and apply to The Rotary Foundation for a Matching Grant to get hydrated food for a needy country—so your rubber chicken lunch will today lead to a $42,000 commitment to alleviate hunger in a place where people think of hunger not as pangs between breakfast and lunch, but as a cause of death every day."

There was more applause.

"The sergeants at arms will direct your tables in an orderly fashion to the six serving stations. When you return to your seats, you will notice a printed card in the middle of the table. Please use that as the subject for your luncheon conversation. Each of those topics: children at risk, hunger, safe drinking water, medical services, avoidable blindness, education, help for the aging, peacemaking, protecting planet Earth, ... and I'm missing one, I think ... each will have a separate one-hour workshop immediately following this luncheon if you would like to gain—or contribute—more information on the subject. So *bon appetit*, and have many healthy, constructive conversations."

My table was one of the first to be invited to serve ourselves, and we were soon back in our seats with an excellent beef barley soup, crusty French bread roll, and crisp garden salad. There were seven others at my table, none of whom I had met previously. One was Harriet, the incumbent governor of the district in which this hotel was located. Another was a florist named Felice, and an airline pilot—Phil, and others whom I would come to know in the next hour.

"Well, let us see what we have been assigned," said Harriet, reaching for the folded card in the center of the table. She opened it, studied it for a moment, and announced to her expectant audience: "*Peace. The Rotary Foundation's contribution to peace.*"

"Quite a challenge," declared Phil. "I suppose if we need to bring about world peace in ..." he looked at his watch "... fifty minutes, we'd better skip dessert!"

We all laughed.

"What do you all think about Rotary's ability to facilitate peace?" asked Harriet.

There was the silence that typically prevails at the beginning of a discussion group, when nobody really wants to lead the discourse. Finally, one of the members who had not previously introduced himself spoke up.

"Forgive me if I'm wrong, but I'm quite new to Rotary. I am only here today because my club president thought this conference would help me better understand what Rotary represents. However, from my perspective, I never thought of Rotary as much of an *international* organization. I think of the Rotary club as the nice folks who put up park benches and take handicapped kids to the zoo. They are the people who have the pancake breakfast; Rotary doesn't have anything to do with bringing about world peace, does it?"

"Excuse me, what is your name?" The question came from a rather elderly man of apparent Asian heritage wearing a name badge with "Fumio" on it.

"Sorry, I'm Bill Lambert, from the Queensborough Rotary Club. I think I must have dropped my name badge this morning," explained the first speaker.

"Bill, I am very pleased to meet you. I'm Fumio, and as you can see ..." he tapped his engraved name badge "... many years ago, I was district governor. My parents were both born in Japan. And as proud, hard-working, honest Americans, when I was a teenager living in California, we were all captured and forced to live in an internment camp during World War Two. Seventeen of my close family members, including all four of my grandparents, died when the atomic bomb exploded over Hiroshima."

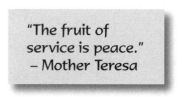

"The fruit of service is peace."
– Mother Teresa

He took a sip of tea while we waited for him to continue.

"Now I am not telling you this because I want to make *me* a part of this story, but to show you how I have been so tragically impacted by war. My brother was a U.S. Marine who was killed in Korea. I lost a son over Vietnam when his airplane exploded. But here is the point: by the time Hiroshima and Nagasaki hit the headlines, *Rotary* was already established as a major influence in bringing people together to use mutual friendships and understanding as a way of avoiding conflict."

"I had no idea," said Felice. "How so?"

"During the Second World War, Rotarians in England began organizing groups of influential refugees to help plan how to restore civil order once the shooting stopped," Fumio continued. "That group was later formalized as the United Nations Educational, Scientific and Cultural Organization: UNESCO. Isn't that right, Frank?"

"It sure is," I agreed. "And speaking of the United Nations, many Rotarians were among those who drafted—and signed—the organizing documents chartering the U.N. And the U.N. Declaration of Human Rights was adopted almost verbatim from Rotary's Declaration of Human Rights that we wrote back in 1942."

"Haven't there been cases where Rotarians literally helped bring peace between warring countries?" asked a middle-aged man with a badge indicating his name was 'Chuck.'

"Well, Chuck, the easy answer to your question is 'Yes.' There have been many occasions—several I can recall in Latin America—when either actual conflict or imminent hostilities were ended by Rotarians from both nations who brought the people from all sides together around a table and brokered a peaceful resolution.

"But to me, the most eloquent spokesperson for Rotary's essential role as a peacemaker is someone who shares your first name." Chuck looked startled. "His name is Charles C. Keller—but the Rotary world knows him as Chuck. He was president of Rotary International in 1987 and 1988 and he made peace a key theme of his presidential year—and of all the years since. I vividly recall Chuck saying that Rotary has no army; it has no guns and no power to prosecute or punish. Rotary even prides itself on being totally free of sectarian and political opinions. So how could such an organization be an effective peacemaker?"

I realized all seven members were looking intently at me, now wanting the answer to Chuck's hypothetical question.

"His argument is that those powers: the might of an army, the threat of a weapon, the punishment of a judicial system, are powers that *externally* enforce peace. Rotary's strength is that it has, for over one hundred years, worked to achieve peace *internally*. By fostering understanding between people of different ethnic or religious backgrounds, by reducing hunger and suffering, and by increasing their self sufficiency, they see hope in the future—and tensions with their once-perceived enemies are reduced."

"The year I was district governor, the tensions between Palestinians and Israelis were so heightened that the world expected another Middle East war to erupt at any moment," Fumio recalled. "When all the incoming governors went for our ten-day training conference, one of my classmates had an incredible project. All thirteen clubs in Israel put together a job training program for disadvantaged Palestinian teenagers—and The Rotary Foundation gave them a Matching Grant of $20,000 to make it possible."

"Excuse my skepticism, but that hasn't exactly brought peace and tranquility to the region, has it?" asked a stern looking woman called Alice.

"No, it hasn't," Fumio agreed. "But let's say there were one hundred youths that were helped in that program in the first year. Those kids are now in their late thirties or early forties. While some of their peers paint all Israelis as the enemy, these men and women have different perceptions. They remember the Israeli Rotarians who mentored them and spent hundreds of hours helping them, giving them a real chance at learning the skills to find and hold good jobs. I know some of those Rotarians even gave them some seed money to start their own businesses.

"Meanwhile, on the other side of the border, when Israelis condemn all Palestinians as murderous terrorists, those Rotarians who have had warm, personal relationships with Palestinians in the job training program know them to be trustworthy, friendly, and peace loving. In the big scheme of things, when you look at the entire population of Israel and Palestine, the one hundred Arabs and one hundred Israelis involved in that program do not amount to much. However, it is a start. And the next year, another one hundred went through the program, a year later, another hundred. So a decade later, you have one thousand people from each side who, chances are, do not paint the other side as automatically all being the enemy. Now imagine if each of those one thousand people who have been through that one little Rotary program can each speak to their spouses, their children, their families and friends. They can be advocates of tolerance and mutual understanding, correcting them when they use racist or inflammatory comments about the other side with their own personal testimonies about their experience with them. Now you have a force of thousands who might stop painting them with the broad brush of hatred, and maybe, just maybe, many of those people might be prepared to give peace a chance."

> "If world understanding and peace are going to be achieved, it is important that I do my part by supporting The Rotary Foundation with my endeavors and financial contributions. Let there be peace on earth, and let it begin with me."
> – John E. Hinrichs, Rotary Club of Scotia, New York, USA, District 7190

"Fumio, I really appreciate your words," said Harriet. "You have brought home to us how each person here can make peace a personal mission. Every year, our district has a multi-faith prayer breakfast, and we always end the event by linking arms and singing, *Let there be peace on earth, and let it begin with me*. Without fail, I am deeply moved to see Christians, Moslems, Jews, and Buddhists—and, I suppose, agnostics—united by both physical and vocal bonds as they sing that song. It is so easy for us to assume that peacemaking is somebody else's job: the president's, or the U.N's, or the responsibility our elected national leaders. What you have brought home, to me at least, is that *I* can be a peacemaker just by being more proactive through Rotary."

"I don't want to seem to be the negative voice here, because I, too, want to be part of the solution," said Alice. "I was also quite moved by what I have heard here today. But how can *I*, Alice, as one ordinary person, be a part of that solution?"

"Frank, why don't you handle that one?" said Harriet, in less of a suggestion than a directive.

"Sure." I began, quickly thinking of the best way to do so. "Let me ask you to consider two restaurants. The first is right here. I know we had a special lunch today, but ordinarily, the server would place before you a set meal. Even if the conference organizers had ordered a five-course dinner, we would all be served exactly the same food, at the same time and with the same level of service. But I noticed as we were unloading the car last night that right across the street is a cafeteria-style restaurant. If we were to eat there, we could individually choose whatever food we like most—and could forever avoid the food we don't like."

"Like broccoli?" asked Chuck.

"Like broccoli!" I answered. "But not right now. Remember, we are having an austerity lunch. Just be grateful you did not get cream of broccoli soup." Chuck raised his hands in agreement.

"What I want you to think of is that The Rotary Foundation is your cafeteria plan for serving mankind—and specifically in your role as peacemakers.

Rotary does not serve you a set choice with the only option being 'take it or leave it.' Imagine a continuum of hands-on involvement. At one end, you do not feel as passionate about peacemaking as our friend Fumio here does—but you know you should do *something* to advance the cause of peace. Therefore, you donate to The Rotary Foundation, with the gift designated to a peace project, such as the Peace Scholar program.

"At the other end of the continuum, you and your family endow a permanent scholarship for a new Peace Scholar every two years. Alternatively, perhaps you launch your own peacemaking project, enlisting both volunteer and financial support from Rotarians on both sides of a disputed line—and from The Rotary Foundation. Somewhere in the middle might be where you could take a trip, individually, or with a group of like-minded volunteers—to teach specific skills to people in another culture. I have been increasingly alarmed at the recent escalation in the distrust between Christians, Muslims, and Jews. Much of this is fueled by ignorance; all three religions actually have much in common. So perhaps you and your Rotary club could hold a trialogue workshop where leaders from the three faiths could come together, explain to the audience the true beliefs of their religion, and seek to find common ground, mutual respect, and understanding.

"In some of the most deadly conflicts of recent history, combatants have lain down their arms for 'Days of Tranquility' while Rotarians immunized children against polio. Even brutal warlords have changed their rhetoric when they saw our willingness to go into their most blighted impoverished communities to help their neediest citizens.

"Do you see what I mean? Imagine that the cafeteria opens Monday. You have two days to decide what you want to put on your plate. This will be a happy feast!

You do not need to eat the broccoli, unless you want to. So think now—and I would like to just go around the table and ask each of you for the first answer that comes to mind; here's the question: what would *you* like to do to help the world become more peaceful in the future?"

I knew I was taking quite a risk. There were several seconds of silence after my question. Fumio was the first to speak.

"I am very proud of my heritage," he began. "But I am also very aware that Japan's political and military leaders caused destruction and despair in some parts of the world that still causes hatred half a century later. For a couple of years now, I have been aware of how much distrust there still is between Korea and Japan. I would like to develop a group of Koreans and Japanese that could honestly address issues from the past and use the fellowship and trust we have in Rotary to build a new attitude of friendship between our two nations."

"And how would you propose starting such a group?" I asked him.

"I think Rotary is the obvious answer," he said. "Rotary is extremely well respected in both

"Rotary districts that donate a minimum of $25,000 every year, or $50,000 every other year to support the Rotary Centers for International Studies program are recognized as Rotary Centers Peacebuilder Districts. The Rotary Foundation will recognize Peacebuilder Districts with special banners and certificates. For more information, go to www.rotary.org/foundation/educational/amb_scho/funding/index/html

countries. Only the very highest caliber of person may belong to Rotary in Japan and Korea, and since our organization strongly advocates cross-cultural friend-ship and international peace and goodwill, I think the foundation already exists."

"I completely agree," I said. Before anybody else could speak, Sue's voice came across the public ad-dress system, asking delegates to conclude their discussions within the next two minutes.

"We will have to make this fast," said Harriet. "Does anybody have just a few words they would like to add?"

"I am a pediatric nurse practitioner," said Alice. "My husband is a geologist. Our children are both grown; our mortgage is paid off. I have not spoken with Ken about this, but I think we both would be open to the idea of serving in a developing country by sharing our professional skills with people who have no access to them. How can we get more information on those op-portunities to become Rotary volunteers?"

"The quick answer is to suggest you call The Ro-tary Foundation office at 1.847.866.3000. But if you give me your business card, I'll make sure somebody calls you," I promised her.

"Frank, I have an aunt who is now very frail," said Harriet. "She spent the first half of her life as a mis-sionary in East Africa. She led a very frugal life, and after her first husband died and she returned home, she remarried a man who left her quite wealthy when he passed away last year. Aunt Jessica has no chil-dren, and I would like to approach her with the idea of leaving a substantial part of her estate to The Rotary Foundation. I think she would be open to the sug-gestion, especially if she could see her beloved Africa benefit from the bequest."

"Harriet," I said. "That's the *legacy* I spoke of this morning. We can absolutely assure her that her gift to The Rotary Foundation would be the legacy that keeps living on in Africa long after she has passed from this world."

"I feel a bit like the poor kid on the block," Jim interjected. "I don't have a lot of money to leave—and frankly, I wasn't planning on needing to for quite a while anyway. I have a job and a family to support, so I cannot go off for months on end to serve on a peace mission in another country. However, I have had one idea. We have a summer camp in my town that brings in maybe fifty foreign students every summer to work. They come from all over the world. However, the camp only pays them three dollars an hour, and it is so remote that the kids never get to see anything or meet anyone other than the campers or the other workers. So they come over here, work incredibly hard umpteen hours a day for two or three months, then fly home. I think they get a day off every two weeks, but they spend most of that time sleeping or hanging out in their bunk at camp. This may not be much of an idea, but what if my club had an international day every two weeks? We could have members pick the kids up at camp; take them to our homes, or the beach, or a movie, or just fellowship with them. Most of all, if the kid is from, say, Hungary, we could learn about his country in a way we would never have been able to otherwise."

"Jim, that's a wonderful idea!" said Felice. "I'm also from Queensborough, but I am in the morning club. I think we would love to do this as a joint project with your evening club. To me, you have just touched on fellowship, peace through mutual understanding, and international service—all in a single, virtually cost-free program."

A bell clanged loudly from the podium.

"I am afraid our time is up," said Governor Harriet, our table captain. "Frank, do you have any parting words?"

"I don't want to be blamed for making you late for your next workshop," I said. "But two things: first, do let me have your email addresses and I will send you some very valuable Rotary Foundation links. Second, I like the answers you just gave. You proved my point that service along the pathway to peace can be given in many ways. It can be given in a grand and generous form, or it can be delivered in a personal, individual way. However, what is *most* important is what Governor Harriet said: to *think* peacemaking, to commit personally to the pledge, *Let there be peace on earth, and let it begin with me.* I don't know how I could deliver on those words if I were not in Rotary. But The Rotary Foundation gives me not just the will, but the *way* to deliver on my promise."

"Walter Felman, of the Rotary Club of Mill Hill, England, visited a seven-month-old Palestinian girl recovering from heart surgery at a hospital in Holton, Israel. The girl breathed without assistance for 24 hours for the first time in her life, monitored by a servo ventilator, which delivers oxygen and nitric oxide in an emergency. The US$60,000 device was provided to Save a Child's Heart charity through a project of District 1130 (England) and other Rotarians in Great Britain and Ireland, the Rotary Club of Holon, and a Rotary Foundation Matching Grant."
– The Rotary Foundation 2004 report.

"The Global Polio Eradication Initiative is a shining model of how we can all come together against a common enemy of humankind. A final victory is within reach. You are the key to success . . . You can count on the support of the United Nations family and its partners—especially Rotary International."

– UN Secretary, General Kofi Annan at the January 2004 meeting of National Ministers of Health.

## CHAPTER 6

# Ask Not ...

**B**right sunlight streamed through my window, heralding a beautiful new day—although from the way people on the street far below were bundled up and hurriedly moving about, I sensed it must be very cold outside.

I had missed the casual breakfast so that I could catch up on several important email messages with my office in Mexico City. I glanced at my watch and noticed, with great alarm, that it was almost nine o'clock. I had less than five minutes to get downstairs to the opening plenary session—a presentation by none other than my personal Rotary recruit: Bob. I grabbed my jacket, let the door slam behind me, and hurriedly made my way to the elevator. To my relief, it came within seconds.

"Mr. Devlyn! Good morning. I am Tony Bevilacua, Rotary Foundation Chairman of the Woodside Morning Club. How are you today?"

"I am doing well, Tony." I answered. "And how about you?"

"Fine, thank you, sir."

"Hey! None of that *sir* stuff," I warned him. "And you can leave out the *Mister Devlyn*, too. You know Rotarians are on a first-name basis with one another."

"Okay, *Frank*. If you say so."

"Frank, I have to tell you, your talk yesterday morning really served as a call to action for me. I spent much of the rest of the day thinking about my dash, and how to make it more significant. I don't have all the answers yet, but your anecdotes really made the question come alive within me."

I could feel my ears popping as the elevator dropped the 34 floors almost instantly.

"You know, Tony, having you say that reminds me of a story Bhichai Rattakul told me recently. Bhichai served as Rotary International President two years after me, and he was riding in a crowded elevator as it descended a very tall building in New York. As they plunged forty-two floors downward, one of the passengers jokingly asked the elevator operator what would happen if the cable broke. The operator told her that the answer depended on the type of life they had been living."

There was nervous laughter from the three people in my lift—and I think they looked relieved when the doors opened at the conference level a few seconds later. I shook Tony's hand and quickly followed the signs to the Ambassador Ballroom East. As I took my seat, less than a minute before the program was called to order, I felt a particular sense of pride at seeing Bob at the head table. The Regional Rotary Foundation Coordinator introduced him and Bob walked over to the podium.

"Good morning, everyone," he began. A low rumble of responses came from the audience. "I understand that an essential part of accepting membership in Alcoholics Anonymous—or any twelve-step program—is to introduce oneself to one's peers each time with an honest admission of one's weakness. So let me start again. Good morning, everyone. My name is Bob, and I'm a recovering self-centered human being."

He had their attention now. Several audience members, in unison, called back, "Hiya, Bob!"

"I joined Rotary six years ago ... and I believe I became a *Rotarian* more than two years later." He paused to see if the significance of his statement had sunk in. It had.

"I thought my club meetings were boring—and that some of the members were just not people with whom I felt a connection. The truth of it is, I had just about dropped out of Rotary. In retrospect, I now admit that I was looking for what Rotary could do for me, rather than the other way around.

"My life up to that point had focused on money, cars, and having a good time. But as I hit my thirties and began staring at middle age ..."

A cacophony of guffaws and protests briefly interrupted his speech.

"... I got married, was promoted into management, and twin baby girls arrived. Yesterday morning, we heard Frank Devlyn tell us about one extraordinary life: that of Arch Klumph, founder of The Rotary Foundation, and how he had the vision for an endowment fund with the one very simple, but oh-so-worthy objective: *to do good in the world.*

"Why did Arch Klumph join Rotary? We do not know. Why did he agree to become his club's president? Was it for the prestige of the office? Was it because as leader of a group of prominent corporate titans he could sell a lot of lumber? We do not know. In fact, we know little of his motivation for joining Rotary or of how effective he was as a club president.

"But none of that is important now. The real point is that after serving in his local club for quite a while, his eyes opened and his horizons widened. He saw the needs of people less fortunate than himself far from his local community—and he felt the call to help them, too. He used The Rotary Foundation to make that possible.

"Please do not mistake me, ladies and gentlemen. I am not about to compare my Rotary commitment to that of Arch Klumph. What I do want is to make the point that no matter whether we are new or long-time Rotarians, no matter whether we have been active members—or just seat warmers; the best opportunities for us to serve lie in the future."

Applause rippled through the room.

"When Sue asked me to speak today, I was shocked—for a couple of reasons. First, I *hate* public speaking. Second, I am hardly the poster child for acting like a Rotarian. Therefore, instead of thinking of this as a speech, I want it to be just one Rotarian's story. As I mentioned earlier, I joined Rotary six years ago. However, for almost half that period, I drifted into the meetings pretty much if I did not have anything else to do that day. I thought the meetings, and several of the Rotarians, were boring.

"Then Sue—who had become a good friend—became our club's president elect, and right before her presidential year began, we had dinner with Frank Devlyn." He nodded in my direction.

"By the end of that evening, he had persuaded me to give Rotary another chance, and by the time the district conference finished, Sue had roped me into helping her re-energize our club. The following week, she and I had lunch together, and she shared with me her decision to make The Rotary Foundation the focus of her presidential year. I remember asking her, 'What does The Rotary Foundation do?'

"Maybe a couple of weeks later, my boss called me into her office and told me the company was sending me to India for six weeks to oversee the opening of our new computer center in Hyderabad. I had been there before on shorter trips, and the worst part of those assignments is the loneliness you feel in the evenings and at weekends. Sue suggested I contact the local Rotary club in Hyderabad: 'Perhaps you could make up a few meetings with them and make a friend,' she said.

"So I sent maybe half a dozen email enquiries to club presidents I found in Sue's Rotary International Official Directory. The very night I arrived in Hyderabad—I literally had only been in my hotel room for a half-hour—the telephone rang. It was the president of one of the local Rotary clubs, inviting me to join him at their meeting the next evening.

"Folks, have you ever heard that old axiom, *be careful what you wish for*? Never again will I head off to India worried that I might get bored during my free time. I felt so welcome at their club, and I soon became friends with their president, Deepak, He apologized for not inviting me to his home or business right away, explaining that his club, and the other 12 clubs in Hyderabad—indeed, every Rotary club across India—was gearing up for a massive PolioPlus National Immunization Day two weeks later. Almost every waking moment would be devoted to following the incredibly detailed plan of execution. I must admit, my friends, I did not even know what a National Immunization Day was.

"I soon found out! Much of the club's meeting that night was devoted to action reports by various committees charged with reaching every child in the city on the big day. I offered to help distribute pamphlets to the 300 or so workers at our call center. Then one of the other Rotarians said he was concerned about networking a series of laptops they would be using to communicate between immunization posts—so I offered to help there, too. That is the area of my formal training. In the next two weeks, I think I must have spent eight or nine evenings, plus Saturday and much of Sunday, working on the NID.

"And then the big day arrived. I have never experienced anything like that day in my life! They executed it with military precision. Rotarians from throughout the city and across India; no, we even had a bunch of Rotarian volunteers from Australia, Ireland, and Canada—were told where to be and what to do. Everywhere you looked, there were signs and people in yellow PolioPlus hats and tee shirts ... and lines, and lines, and lines of women with their babies. You have heard the term 'teeming masses'? *These* were teeming masses, folks. Moreover, they were all there for one single reason: to take advantage of this incredible opportunity to protect their children's lives that Rotary—*my* Rotary, *your* Rotary—had organized.

"Until that experience, I must admit to you, I had thought of Rotary as a group of people who met for lunch every Tuesday in a mediocre restaurant down the road from my office. That was *my* Rotary universe. It was defined in my eyes by a few nice people and a few whom I did not particularly care for. And what good did Rotary do? They gave a couple of $1,000 scholarships to local kids and planted pretty flowers around the 'Welcome' signs at the entrance to town.

"But suddenly, here were radio messages and hundreds of Rotarians' vans delivering vaccine and thousands of Rotarians corralling their families and employees to immunize—are you ready for this—every child in the second-most-populous nation on earth. They immunized one hundred and fourteen *million* children—and they did it in a *single day*."

Spontaneous applause again resonated throughout the ballroom. Bob nodded his head to acknowledge the response and raised his right hand so he could continue.

"It is easy to become mesmerized by statistics. Indeed, some of the numbers from the PolioPlus Campaign are literally impossible for us to envision. How can we see in our own mind one hundred and fourteen *million* children lining up in a single day? We can read the Rotary Foundation statistics of a ninety-nine percent decline in new polio cases since our campaign began twenty years ago—yet how can the average Rotarian truly feel a sense of ownership in eliminating ninety-nine percent of a global killing disease? I suppose The Rotary Foundation *has to* continually communicate these big numbers to Rotarians around the world. First, they should feel a sense of pride in the incredible success of PolioPlus. Second, the job is not over; Rotary *needs* financial support from every Rotarian in order to finish the job and forever rid the earth of the dreaded scourge of polio.

"But let me tell you the effect the PolioPlus Campaign had on me. India was hot. Oh boy, I cannot tell you how hot it was on the National Immunization Day. I helped wherever the committee needed me, so that meant fixing laptops, carrying heavy boxes of vaccine, distributing water to the volunteer stations. Then came a moment that will be with me for the rest of my life. Deepak, the club president who was the first Indian Rotarian to befriend me, was working at an immunization point when I delivered some cold storage boxes filled with vaccine. 'Hey, Bob," he called. "Why don't you come over here and help for a few minutes. I need a short break."

"I looked over and saw this line of women and children that seemed to stretch forever. It was several hundred yards long. There were grandmothers and teenagers and sometimes entire families—but everyone, *everyone*, came with an infant. 'I don't know what to do,' I told Deepak—who is a pediatrician at a Hyderabad hospital. However, he assured me it was easy, and before I had time to think of another excuse, he took the baby from the young mother at the front of the line and thrust her into my arms. I cradled her as if she were made of eggshells and could break if I held too tightly.

"Deepak gently showed me how to purse her lips, making an opening in her mouth. Then with his encouragement, I squeezed the small container to place two drops of vaccine under her tongue. She was completely still; totally silent. Deepak gestured for me to hand her back to her mother—a young woman I suspect was in her late teens. 'Thank you, sir.' She said to me, a wide smile. 'Thank you for saving my daughter's life.'

"My worldview changed in that moment, fellow Rotarians. When I was holding that little girl in my arms and that vaccine dropper in my hand, I suddenly thought of my own precious twin daughters half a world away back here. They were less than a year old at the time—about the same age as that little girl. I remembered thinking, 'What if there were a dreaded disease that killed and crippled children in *my* neighborhood? What if I was poor and unable to protect my beloved children, and then along came a Rotarian who did not even know their names? And yet he—and a million other Rotarians just like him—made it possible to immunize my little girls so they would never catch that disease?'

"Suddenly, I realized that supporting The Rotary Foundation; by making it *our* foundation, *my* foundation became a priority in my life. I knew from that moment on that by sharing just a small portion of my own financial resources, I could save the lives of thousands of children. Children whose mothers and fathers love them every bit as much as we love *our* sons and daughters; children every bit as beautiful as our own children and grandchildren. In an instant, the statistics of how many millions of people The Rotary Foundation has served became secondary; what The Rotary Foundation really meant to me was *that* little girl, with her big brown eyes looking up at me—and the gratitude of her mother for saving her daughter from death—or a lifetime as a crawler."

Bob stopped to take a sip of water. I glanced around the room and sensed the audience had been intensely moved by his personal testimony. I have often heard it said that there are no coincidences; everything that happens is really part of the plan being orchestrated by our Creator. Could it be so, I wondered, in Bob's case? Here was a man on the point of dropping out of Rotary altogether. Then his company dispatched him on a business trip to the other side of the world, setting up a chain of events that turned him into one of The Rotary Foundation's most enthusiastic, eloquent spokesmen and supporters.

"After the NID was over, I still had almost a month left on my work assignment in India. Deepak had included me in the committee meetings for the NID, so I really did feel a part of a Rotary team. Several other Rotarians befriended me and invited me to make up at their clubs, and even to their homes. Before long, it seemed every weekend—and several weekday evenings—were fully booked as I they introduced me to the work Rotary was doing in India.

"One weekend, I visited a project The Rotary Foundation had just approved for a Matching Grant between Indian Rotarians and those in Mexico. It was in a very poor village maybe an hour outside Hyderabad. Boy, talk about a tale of two cities! There was Hyderabad: a modern, hi-tech, economically thriving metropolis. Then we came to this little village with no paved streets, impoverished people, and no running water. The women had to carry water every day from a filthy, polluted stream. No wonder so many people—especially the children—had contracted serious water-born diseases. Anyway, Rotarians from a nearby town designed a deep-water well and a simple, safe irrigation system that delivers clean drinking water right to a tap in the center of the village. Because much of the work was done by volunteers, the entire project cost only $29,000. Can you imagine? Safe drinking water for an entire village of one thousand people, for only $29,000!

> "Rotary has won a place of respect in the global village; in fact, Rotary has helped make the world a global village."
> – Carol Bellamy, Executive Director, UNICEF

"The local club raised part of that, the Mexican Rotarians came up with almost half the money—and The Rotary Foundation gave them a Matching Grant of $14,000 to complete the project. So your donations—and mine—to the Foundation helped those people by giving them something we all take for granted: safe drinking water—for the rest of their lives.

"The Rotarians in another club I visited were astounded that I had never heard of something called the Jaipur Limb Project—with which they were very involved. This is a local Indian endeavor that began back in 1984 to provide artificial limbs to the poor, both in India and now in countries around the world—especially where there are many victims of land mines and war. Originally, amputees had to travel sometimes thousands of miles to get their limbs from the factory in Jaipur, but local Rotary clubs now hold temporary Limb Camps, at which patients can be fitted with their new legs or arms, and trained how to use them. The club I worked with held a two-week camp and it was an incredible privilege for me to be involved. Technicians from Jaipur attended the camp to assist with the calipers and equipment, and more than one hundred Rotarians worked with the patients. They came in all sizes; young and old, men and women, but they all were so poor that they could never have afforded prostheses without this program, so they had literally become throwaway people, condemned to be crawlers for the rest of their lives. Seven hundred and eighty people received new limbs in the two weeks of our Jaipur Camp. They told me the total cost was $30,000—of which almost 50 percent was funded by a Matching Grant from our Rotary Foundation. Now think about that, my friends. That averages $38 per person! Can you imagine ..."

Bob reached into his pocket and pulled out two $20 bills ... "For thirty-eight bucks, giving a child an artificial leg so she might walk again? Or a man a prosthetic arm so he can now hold a job and provide for his family? How could any decent, caring person *not* want to be a part of this work?"

Bob glanced at his watch.

"I see my time is almost up. I wish I had time to tell you some of the other ways in which I personally witnessed our Foundation's amazing work in India. I wish I could tell you about my two days at the Sightsavers Eye Clinic that Rotarians from England—and a Rotary Foundation grant—made possible. Rotary volunteers brought into the clinic people blinded by cataracts, and I saw those folks literally walk out two days later being able to see. I saw young people—Interactors and Rotaractors—deeply involved in that project, bringing life to what Past Rotary International President Cliff Dochterman pointed out: that real happiness is helping others. Indian Rotarians are able to carry out three- to five cataract sight restorations for only one hundred dollars.

"I wish I had time to tell you about the Saturday when I enlisted some volunteers from my own company to install computers in a special school for the deaf—computers that were purchased through a Matching Grant of The Rotary Foundation with funding from Rotarians in New Zealand.

"Suffice it to say, ladies and gentlemen, that I returned to my club and my district thoroughly convinced that The Rotary Foundation is one of the greatest, most effective forces for good in the world today. Every one of us in this room would say, 'I want to make the world a better place.' That is an empty platitude. The quandary is what good can any of us do alone? How would any one of us be able, by ourselves, to even know about the clean water project, or eye clinic I just described? We would not even know they existed. However, when I give a thousand dollars to make my father a Paul Harris Fellow, I am not only honoring him; I am simultaneously giving The Rotary Foundation the money to fund projects such as those about which I just told you. Moreover, when I make an annual pledge, I multiply the abilities of our Foundation many times over. When I include The Rotary Foundation in my estate planning, I ensure that long after I have passed on, the gift I gave will keep on giving.

"I went to India for my job. Today, I cannot even remember what I did during the workday on that assignment. What was the lasting significance of my work during those six weeks? I don't know. I hope I did a good job, but truthfully, the world is not a better place because of what I did in our Hyderabad call center. However, look at what a difference I can make by participating in The Rotary Foundation projects, both as a hands-on volunteer and as a contributor to help keep its programs going. President John F. Kennedy challenged us to 'Ask not what your country can do for you; ask what you can do for your country.' As Rotarians, should we not ratchet that up to the next level and ask, 'What can I do for my fellow man and for the world?'

"My fellow Rotarians, I can still see the eyes of that precious little girl to whom I gave the polio vaccine. She will never know my name, or even what I did. But she could grow up to be a scientist, a doctor, a peacemaker who profoundly changes her society for the better. And she will do so because Rotarians like you, and me, made the personal commitment not just to care, but to take this Rotary Foundation and make it *our* Rotary Foundation, and to support it generously and regularly. Thank you for your attention."

The audience erupted into applause, rising to give Bob a standing ovation. He looked surprised—even a little embarrassed—at the accolade. As the applause subsided, I felt enormously proud of Bob. He had connected with the audience by not doing what many local Rotary Foundation spokespeople do. Too often, they focus on the money. Bob had personalized The Rotary Foundation by focusing on the people it serves. He personified an old axiom of salesmanship: in order to be convincing, you have to be convinced.

At the Seattle Special Olympics, nine contestants, all physically or mentally disabled, assembled at the starting line for the 100-yard dash. At the gun, they all started out, not exactly in a dash, but with a relish to run the race to the finish and win. All, that is, except one little boy who stumbled on the asphalt, tumbled over a couple of times, and began to cry. The other eight heard the boy cry. They slowed down and looked back. Then they all turned around and went back . . . every one of them. One girl with Down's Syndrome bent down, kissed him, and said, "This will make it better." Then all nine linked arms and walked together to the finish line. Everyone in the stadium stood; the cheering went on for several minutes. People who were there are still telling the story. Why? Because deep down we know this one thing: What matters in life is more than winning for ourselves. What matters in this life is helping others win, even if it means slowing down, and changing our course.

– as told by Eddie Blender

## CHAPTER 7

# Open Forum

"**F**rank! Frank! Do you have a moment, please?" It was Sue, and from the distraught look on her face, I could tell she had a problem.

"Sure," I answered, "What's up?"

"Let's talk out in the hallway while Bob answers the audience questions," she suggested, moving towards the nearest doors.

"Oh, Frank! I had everything so well planned for this entire conference—right down to the smallest detail. Now I just got a call from MaryAnn Evans. She was to be our next speaker. She was here at lunchtime, but apparently ran out to the computer store to get a new bulb for the projector she planned to use for her presentation. On the way back here, some chap ran a red light and hit her car."

"Is she all right?" I asked.

"Thankfully, yes. She sounds shaken up and says she is very sore, but was not seriously injured. However, her car has to be towed. There is no way she can make it back on time—and I have 580 Rotarians expecting to be inspired by MaryAnn's presentation."

"Could somebody else make the presentation for her," I wondered aloud.

"No. It was to be a personalized program using her own photographs. Poor MaryAnn. She said her laptop and projector were broken in the crash too when they slammed into the dashboard."

"Is there anything I can do to help?" I inquired.

"Yes. That is why I sought you out. I grabbed my co-chair a few minutes ago and we have an idea. MaryAnn was supposed to follow Bob—in 10 minutes. Then Jim McCleary was to follow her for a 30-minute session on which forms to use for various Rotary Foundation applications and programs. I am going to ask him to switch spots with MaryAnn, and go on at three o'clock. That gives us ...' she glanced at her watch "... about 25 minutes to come up with a replacement program."

"Any ideas?" I asked.

"Actually, yes!" she replied, with a slight smile. "I thought we could hold an open forum, where folks could ask questions on any Rotary Foundation subject, and you and a couple of others I might be able to rope in—could answer them. Please, Frank! In all my meticulous planning of the conference, I had not anticipated something like this, and I cannot have a 45-minute hole in the middle of the afternoon program."

"Of course I'll help," I assured her. Just tell me where you want me to be and when you want me to be there."

She looked at her watch again. "Why don't you plan to be right there, at the head table, at ten minutes to four? I will speak to Ernie Perkins, our Regional Rotary Foundation Coordinator and try to recruit him. If I think of anyone else, I will let you know. By the time you go on, we'll have a microphone in front of each of you and a couple of floor mikes in the aisles out there for questions."

"Sounds like you have already put your Plan B into action," I said. "Remember the theme I chose for my Rotary International presidential year: Create Awareness, Take Action. You have done both in this conference so far, Sue. Relax. Everything will be just fine."

"Thanks, Frank." She said, touching my arm gratefully. "Perhaps you would prefer to spend the next 20 minutes in the peace of your room, where you could prepare an outline. You know how nobody likes to jump right in with the first question at the beginning. Maybe you would want to lead off with some thoughts on what you have heard as the most often-asked questions, or most misunderstood issues in The Rotary Foundation, and that might stimulate more questions from the audience."

I appreciated her suggestion and headed back to my room, picking up a cup of coffee on the way. Promptly at 3:50, I was back in the ballroom. As I walked behind the head table, the Regional Rotary Foundation Coordinator greeted me effusively.

"Hello again, Frank. We have both been so busy today that I have only had the opportunity to wave to you. It is good to see you again; thanks so much for being here."

"It has been a pleasure," I told him. "I looked for you yesterday, but they told me you could not come until today."

"That's right," he confirmed. "At the last minute I was invited to make a major gifts presentation to a couple in another district. They are leaving for a long

> "Don't throw away your tomorrow! When do people throw away their tomorrow? When opportunities are passed by."
> – Dr. Robert Schuller

cruise today, so they said I must either visit yesterday, or wait for two months until they return. Needless to say, I went yesterday."

"Carpe diem, eh?"

"Indeed."

"How did you do?"

"I think it went very well. They made a verbal commitment to donate a piece of property that is worth about $600,000. And they will also include The Rotary Foundation in a charitable remainder trust that will probably give us another million dollars or so when they pass away."

I was in the midst of congratulating Ernie when the sergeant at arms approached. "Gentlemen, would you please take your seats," he asked. "The room is filling up and we should be ready to start in two or three minutes. Sue asked me to reintroduce you both."

Ernie and I walked over to the table and sat behind the two tent cards on which our names were printed boldly. As the last few stragglers hurried into the room carrying coffee cups, the sergeant at arms began speaking from the lectern.

"Fellow Rotarians, we have had a small program change. MaryAnn Evans was to have been our next presenter. Unfortunately, she was in a car accident a couple of hours ago. I am happy to report that MaryAnn is fine, but her car was badly damaged and she was not able to be here. Rotarians are nothing if not flexible, so two of The Rotary Foundation's best spokesmen, Frank Devlyn, chairman the Board of Trustees, and Ernie Perkins, our Regional Rotary Foundation Coordinator, have graciously stepped in to help. Rather than a preplanned presentation, we want this to be *your* time. Have you not always had a question about The Rotary Foundation you wanted answered? Do you have a pet peeve, or a suggestion? Perhaps there is a Rotary Foundation program you would like to have explained better, or know a little more about? Well, folks, this is your chance! There are microphones in each of those two aisles, so step right up and please indicate whether your question is specifically directed at Ernie or President Frank."

"*Buenos Dias*, Señor Frank." The first questioner addressed me in perfect, albeit heavily accented Spanish. "My name is Hector Lopez. I have lived here for almost twenty years, but come from Honduras. Now my club has asked me to be our Rotary Foundation chairperson. We have not been very active in the Foundation before, so I was wondering, are you aware of any Rotary Foundation programs in Honduras?"

"*Hola*, Hector," I began, quickly trying to think back to the details of a Matching Grant that one of the Rotary Foundation staffers had told me about just a week or so earlier.

"I don't know if you aware of the fact that Honduras has the highest rate of AIDS in Central America. It has become a terrible blight there, striking down entire families, since there are very few facilities or medicines to help HIV AIDS victims. A Rotarian from Ohio went to Honduras as a volunteer to help rebuild the country after Hurricane Mitch devastated it back in 1998. However, while he was there, he discovered the AIDS problem, and began exploring with Rotarians from Tegucigalpa the possibility of an AIDS hospice specifically for children with HIV AIDS.

"He touched others with his vision and soon Rotarians in Honduras, Ohio, and Michigan joined together to help found Montaña de Luz—Mountain of Light—a hospice to provide specialized medical care for twenty infected children. The Rotary Foundation gave them a $25,000 Matching Grant, and those children can now live in Montaña de Luz and receive around-the-clock care. It has grown into an amazing project, with volunteers often raising money, collecting medical supplies, and even traveling to Honduras to help. There was a wonderful story about it in *The Rotarian* a couple of years ago.[1] I am sure there are opportunities for you and your club to partner with these other clubs and direct your efforts to Honduras. It would give you all a real sense of identifying with something personal, rather than just asking for donations to a generic cause."

A middle-aged rather matronly-looking woman raised her hand and began speaking. "Good afternoon. My name is Esther Hanson and I have two questions. First, I think these Ambassadorial Scholarships are a wonderful way of teaching goodwill and appreciation of other cultures to young people. But how many students does Rotary send out each year? And my second question concerns something I believe Sue touched on yesterday. She talked about low-income scholarships. How do they differ from the regular Rotary Foundation scholarships?"

"I can take that one," Ernie offered. "Currently, The Rotary Foundation sends approximately 750 Ambassadorial Scholars every year. It is easy to fall into the trap of seeing this as a two-dimensional exchange, meaning students from our country to another, and from other countries to ours. We have to remember that these 750 scholars criss-cross the globe. Koreans are studying in France; Portuguese in South Africa, Sri Lankans in Australia—and so on. This is truly a *global* scholarship program.

---

[1] November 2004 page 37

"As to your second question, The Rotary Foundation sets aside certain funds to provide higher education in world-class universities for students from low-income developing nations. Those people can then take the skills and techniques they learned as a Rotary Foundation scholar and use them to raise the level of knowledge back in their home countries. There is also a Rotary Foundation program that works the other way around. University teachers in developed countries can apply for a grant to teach abroad in an academic field of practical use to people in a low-income developing country."

"President Frank, I have a question about PolioPlus. I have heard all sorts of dates about when we began this program. Which one is right? Oh, and I thought we were supposed to have finished the job in time for Rotary's centennial in 2005. When are we going to complete the job?"

> The Rotary Club of München International, Germany, financed the construction of three houses in Baan Pru-Teow in Krabi, Thailand, as part of a large-scale initiative to build 276 houses and roads in devastated towns. The project is funded by Rotarians worldwide, who have donated more than US$1,925,386.

"I can understand why you may feel there are conflicting dates as to when Rotary's polio eradication campaign began," I admitted. "That is because at first, it was part of our 3H—Health, Hunger, and Humanity—program. In 1979, Rotary launched a five-year project to immunize six million children in The Philippines against polio. When we subsequently decided to make it a global eradication campaign, Rotary called the program Polio 2005. The campaign was renamed PolioPlus and a three-year fundraising effort began in 1985—culminating in the incredible result announced at the Rotary International Convention in 1988, when we announced $247 million in donations and pledges.

"You are right; our goal was to have the job completed by 2005. However, our efforts were hampered by circumstances beyond our control. As polio became virtually extinct, many pharmaceutical companies stopped manufacturing the vaccine. As the supply dropped, the remaining manufacturers dramatically raised their prices. But the biggest obstacles were war and misinformation. Some polio endemic countries had civil wars that prevented us from immunizing every at-risk child. Others spread rumors that the polio vaccine would cause their child to be sterile, and so we were forbidden to conduct NIDs in those regions. As civil wars in places like sub-Saharan Africa caused people to escape the conflict, the unprotected carriers took the poliovirus into neighboring countries that had been polio free.

"By and large, all those problems have now been overcome and we are able to go virtually anywhere on earth with PolioPlus. Here is the bottom line: when we started PolioPlus, there were 125 countries where polio cases were still occurring. Today, we have immunized more than two *billion* children since 1985 and worldwide polio cases have declined by more than 99 percent. By mid-2006, there were only two countries on earth where the poliovirus was still endemic: India and Nigeria. We *will*, let me repeat to you, my friends, The Rotary Foundation *will* eliminate polio from the face of the earth—probably within the next 24 months."

There was an explosive round of applause from the audience, not, I am certain, for me, but for the program to which all Rotarians felt so committed.

"I guess it is Ernie's turn," said the next questioner. "Ernie, going back to the Ambassadorial Scholarships for a moment. My daughter is studying Russian and majoring in international affairs. How could she apply for an Ambassadorial Scholarship?"

Ernie drew his microphone closer. "Are you a Rotarian?" he asked.

"Yes." The woman replied.

"Well I am very sorry, but she cannot qualify. Rotarians and their blood relatives are not eligible for Rotary Foundation scholarships—or to be GSE team members, incidentally."

"That doesn't seem fair," the questioner objected. "After all, *we're* the ones putting the money into the program."

"Speaking of not fair, how come Frank gets the warm and fuzzy PolioPlus question and I get this one?" Ernie said. The audience chuckled. "But seriously, think about it *this* way: when you donate to The Rotary Foundation, you are doing two things. First, you are putting tangible substance behind your pledge as a Rotarian to offer Service Above Self. Second, in many countries, you are giving to a *charitable* foundation and taking a tax deduction for doing so. If you were to benefit from that donation it would be self serving and no longer a charitable gift."

The woman at the microphone nodded as if to accept the explanation and walked back to her seat. Meanwhile, another Rotarian tapped the other microphone to see if it was working.

"I am an accountant." He announced. "I was wondering if either of you could tell us what percentage of The Rotary Foundation's income is spent on administrative expenses."

"Since I did not have advance notice of these questions, I cannot give you the precise details down to the last dollar," I explained. "But I think I can give you the numbers that are pretty close. For the 2003-2004 fiscal year, we had total revenues of about $180 million, and all administrative and fund development costs were about $16.5 million. So that was, what, about nine percent. This past year—2004-2005—total revenues were a little more than $160 million, and total administrative and fund development expenses totaled less than $18 million. Over the past 10 years, 87 percent of The Rotary Foundation's spending has been on our actual programs, with nine percent going to fund development and just four percent for general administrative expenses. As an accountant, I am sure you are aware that consumer agencies in both North America and Europe advise the public to donate to charitable organizations that spend at least 65 percent of their income of their programs. You can see why we are so proud of The Rotary Foundation's stewardship, since it spends 87 percent on actual program support."

"Frank, would you please explain what PolioPlus *Partners* are. Why do we need a separate program from PolioPlus when it seems to me they are both tasked with achieving the same objective."

"We used to get that question a lot," I explained. "Think of the PolioPlus Campaign as the 'big picture.' The original campaign raised the money to buy the vaccine and to work alongside national governments and our partners—WHO, UNICEF, and the CDC—to identify all the children in those countries where the wild poliovirus is still prevalent. The PolioPlus Campaign money pays for the vaccine, but to conduct an effective National Immunization Day—like the one Bob told us about earlier—we need a massive mobilization effort.

"For example, for weeks in advance of the NID, we will advertise the big day on radio, billboards, and in millions of local-language flyers. We even organize puppet shows and video vans—whatever it takes to get out the message. It is critically important for us to reach every parent of appropriately-aged children and to communicate to them the message that they *must* bring their children to the NID. We buy special hats and tee shirts or jackets that clearly identify our volunteers as being NID workers. We must buy special cold storage boxes, and sometimes rent refrigerated trucks to transport the vaccine in safe condition to the thousands of immunization stations. Typically, Rotarians in the local countries donate their own vehicles, but we have dozens of instances where Rotary volunteers had to travel by motorbike, helicopter, and dugout canoe— even by camel— to reach *every* child in even the remotest village. Sometimes, we need a field surveillance laboratory so we can very quickly perform follow-up tests and can watch any unprotected groups in what we call 'mop up operations' before they go on to re-infect other children. All of these are examples of expenses not covered by PolioPlus, but can be provided through your gifts to PolioPlus Partners.

"One final point: you can make a direct gift personally, or as a club or district. Alternatively, you can use your DDF—District Designated Funds—to make a PolioPlus Partners donation."

"Hello there. I must say, for a session that was thrown together at a moment's notice, I am finding this really interesting. My question is, does The Rotary

Foundation do anything to help natural disasters? I always see organizations like the Red Cross and Salvation Army getting lots of publicity after an earthquake or hurricane, but I never see any involvement from Rotary."

I gestured to Ernie for him to take the question, and he seemed willing to do so.

"For the most part, you are right," he said. In a few cases when there were massive needs, such as the Tsunami, or Hurricane Katrina, The Rotary Foundation gave millions of dollars through either Humanitarian Grants or Donor Advised Funds. However, like any well-managed organization, Rotary and The Rotary Foundation needs to recognize what are our strengths—what we do well and what we do not. We cannot be all things to all people. The Rotary Foundation just does not have the staff or the infrastructure to launch immediate disaster relief responses; we do not have warehouses full of tents and blankets, ready to be airlifted somewhere at a moment's notice. Of course, local Rotary clubs and districts where the disaster occurs *are* able to call on the worldwide fellowship of other Rotary clubs for assistance—and they do. That is then channeled through World Community Service or some other similar *Rotary International* program, rather than the Rotary Foundation. Am I right, Frank?"

"Absolutely." I affirmed. "And Rotary International will actively assist those local clubs and districts in sending messages around the Rotary world. I remember the three terrible disasters that occurred at the end of 2005. Many of you will remember the earthquake which struck India and Pakistan that October—killing over 80,000 people. Next Hurricanes Stan and Wilma devastated South Florida and Central America, leaving tens of thousands without homes.

Then-Rotary International president Carl-Wilhelm Stenhammar sent a letter to our family of Rotary asking for help, and over $400,000 came in within days. The same thing happened after the 1999 earthquake in Turkey, and with countless famines, floods, and other natural disasters around the world."

"Ernie, when I first joined Rotary, the ultimate gift we could make was one thousand dollars to The Rotary Foundation, in return for which we got to wear a Paul Harris pin. Now I come to an event like this and see people wearing all sorts of Paul Harris pins. Some have blue stones, some white ones, others have red stones. What is the significance of all these pins nowadays?"

"I am glad you asked." The affable Ernie answered. "The Rotary Foundation wants to recognize the generosity of its donors any time they contribute increments of a thousand dollars or more to our foundation for current use, such as the Annual Programs Fund. Therefore, the pin you got was for your first thousand. Now let us say a couple of years pass and you would like to donate another thousand. Maybe you would like to use it to make your father—who brought you into Rotary—a Paul Harris Fellow. Now *he* gets a Paul Harris Fellow pin, and because you have contributed two thousand dollars altogether, you will receive a new pin with a sapphire on it. A couple of years go by and you make your wife a Paul Harris Fellow. Now she gets a Paul Harris pin, and you get a new one with two sapphires.

"The sapphires continue to surround your pin until you have given six thousand dollars—so by this time, you have a pin with five sapphires. Are you with me? The pin for the first thousand, then five additional one-thousand-dollar gifts added five sapphires, so that takes you up to $6,000. When your total giving to The

Rotary Foundation reaches the seven thousand dollar point, you get a new pin, and this time, it has a ruby on it. Once again, for each thousand you give—even though you may be naming other people as Paul Harris Fellows—the Foundation recognizes *you* by awarding an additional ruby on your own pin. You can accrue up to three rubies, which now recognizes you as a person who has donated $9,000 to our Foundation.

> "Rotary today is an incredible example of how the obstacles of bureaucracy and intolerance can be overcome through good senses and goodwill. It is proof that great things can be accomplished when enough people set their minds to it."
> – William B. Boyd, 2006-2007 President, Rotary International, at 2006 International Assembly.

"But it hardly stops there. By giving ten thousand dollars or more, you have entered the special group of supporter we know as major donors. At ten thousand dollars, you receive a pin with one diamond on it. Level Two major donors, who have reached $25,000 in lifetime cumulative donations, get a two-diamond pin, Level Three donors, having given $50,000, receive a three-diamond pin. Four diamonds indicate $100,000, five diamonds, $500,000, and the top level of supporters—Level Six— receive a pin with six diamonds for contributing one million dollars or more. So if you see somebody wearing one of these pins, be sure to say thank you for making such a difference in our world. And if you would like to *have* one of them, let me buy you dinner tonight!"

"Ladies and gentlemen, we have time for maybe two more questions." The sergeant at arms caused me to look at my watch. It was hard to believe the session was almost over. So much for coming with prepared questions in case nobody wanted to ask their own!

"I have a question...or maybe it is more of a comment." I recognized the questioner as Harriet, the district governor who had been at my table at lunch. "When I was at the International Assembly, being trained with other governors from around the world, I had two governors-elect from Europe at my table. One was from Sweden and the other from Scotland. Anyway, they told me that they do not *allow* Rotarians to make themselves Paul Harris Fellows. One of them said if a Rotarian gave a thousand dollars and asked to be named a Paul Harris, it would be frowned upon. Is that right? How can we expect the sort of financial support you are asking of us from the worldwide body of Rotary if these attitudes prevail?"

Ernie spoke first. "This has been a bit of a problem for The Rotary Foundation for years," he began. "We have to recognize that each club is autonomous and Rotary International and The Rotary Foundation have no power to mandate such things as giving levels or donor recognition—and we don't really want such power. However, the heart of the problem goes back many decades and to cultural differences. Let me make one thing clear: nobody in those countries suggests that their members do not support The Rotary Foundation every bit as much as we do here. The only disparity is in the recognition. Some countries view a Paul Harris Fellow as an *award*, so if you think about it, it is totally inappropriate for one to give an award to himself. The Rotary Foundation has been quietly trying to change that misconception to show that it is not an award but a *recognition*, and it is perfectly normal and appropriate for one to be recognized for his or her generosity. Nevertheless, it can take a long time to change a longstanding belief, and we have to be very careful not to create the appearance of being the Americans *telling* them to do things our way!

"I remember having breakfast with a fellow Regional Rotary Foundation Coordinator from England at a training meeting last year. This very subject came up. He said a member of his club had enjoyed a rather successful year in his business and wanted to give the equivalent of three thousand dollars to The Rotary Foundation—designating himself, his wife, and his daughter as Paul Harris Fellows. His club president told him that he could name his family members but not himself. The Rotarian insisted, at which point the president told him that this was an attitude incompatible with the "Service Above Self" motto of Rotarians, and that he might be asked to leave the club if he continued with this stand. Of course, this was an utterly ridiculous position to take. Can you imagine throwing a good man out of Rotary for giving three thousand dollars to the Foundation? The RRFC who told me this story became involved and he said the problem was not that the man was giving the money—they were very grateful for that; it was that he was claiming the "award" for himself. We at The Rotary Foundation just need to do a better job of communicating with people in the countries where these attitudes exist. We will not change them overnight, but I believe a combination of education and motivation will ultimately help them see the situation for what it really is: an opportunity to recognize Rotarians for their extraordinary support of our wonderful programs."

"President Frank, I have a two-part question. The first is, how can our club find out about Matching Grant opportunities? I think we are ready to do an international service project, but I do not know where to find one. The second part of my question concerns accountability. How can we be sure our money will not go into the pockets of corrupt officials in the receiving country?"

"Let me take your questions one at a time," I said. "You can check out the World Community Service projects at www.rotary.org—and find which clubs are looking for help. Many of these requests could be converted into Matching Grants opportunities. I am sure Ernie here will also be happy to talk to you during our final break. In addition, District 5340 created a great website: www.MatchingGrants.org that I personally recommend. It has details of hundreds of Matching Grant projects in numerous countries.

"As to your second question, few issues are of greater importance to all of us—from the grassroots individual Rotarian to the highest Rotary International officer—than that of transparency and honesty in how our funds are handled. Remember, we have had a half-century of dealing with thousands of grant making situations in every country on earth. The Rotary Foundation *knows* how to verify, and then double check and then triple check every dime they spend. Furthermore, they are not just sending out blank checks from Evanston on a wing and a prayer. The local club, district governor, district Foundation chair, and district subgrants chair are involved and must oversee the entire project and prove that every expense is legitimate. Incidentally, I was in Sri Lanka in 2005 and they showed me a shining example of this transparency. Their website, Rotary-srilanka.org, shows every minute detail for each Rotary Foundation project they are working on. You can literally see the amount of each payment, when it was made, for what purpose, and they provide the telephone and email addresses of the club president, district coordinator, and project manager. So if my club is partnering with a club in Sri Lanka to, say, rebuild a school destroyed by the Tsunami, even though I am in Mexico, I can check on the project's progress on a daily basis and see how the money I have sent them is being spent. And every 15 days, they post digital pictures on the site showing how construction is progressing.

"Of course, the host district and club have to do a lot more than that to get everything approved by The Rotary Foundation, but this is just one small example of how they are also transparent with the donors—or anybody else who might be interested. It is what we all *should* be doing. After all, long before we had a Rotary Foundation, we Rotarians were carrying the flag of business ethics and personal integrity in our business and personal lives."

The sergeant at arms took the microphone at the lectern. "Ladies and gentlemen, that concludes this session. Many thanks for your participation. I hope you found it helpful. If you have any questions, I am sure Frank and Ernie would be happy to answer them during the break. We will now take a very brief intermission. Please be back here in ten minutes for a very inspiring trip around the world—literally. This session is adjourned."

While scouting locations for his film "Apocalypto," Mel Gibson came upon a near apocalyptic situation in southern Mexico: the aftermath of Hurricane Stan.

The storm ripped through the states of Chiapas and Veracruz in October, killing 15 people and displacing 370,000, according to the United Nations Office for the Coordination of Humanitarian Affairs.

Gibson met with Mexican President Vicente Fox and told him he would donate US$1 million to help families rebuild, with one condition: He would make the donation through The Rotary Foundation of Rotary International.

The Hollywood actor and director learned of Rotary from several of his relatives who had traveled with members of the Rotary Club of Tarzana Encino, California, USA, on medical missions to Central America. Gibson and his wife, Robyn, were impressed that The Rotary Foundation had matched their family members' donation to participate.

"The key in their minds [to] the money coming [through] Rotary is that they felt it would be responsibly handled," says Clare Short, of the Tarzana Encino club.

Following the Gibsons' donation, the Foundation set up a hurricane disaster recovery committee, along the lines of similar national committees appointed after the South Asia tsunami, to oversee rebuilding efforts.

## CHAPTER 8

# Trip Around the World

It hardly seemed like more than a few seconds had passed when the sergeant at arms was gaveling the next session to order. In the ten minutes that separated the two presentations, Ernie and I had been peppered with questions from a group of Rotarians who had besieged us. By the time we sat in the front row, Duncan had already been introduced and was approaching the lectern.

Good afternoon," he began. "I have been asked to cut my time short today as we are running a little late and I understand a large group of you will be traveling back to the Washington and Springfield area on the six o'clock train.

"I spent my entire working life—43 years—as a chemical engineer with DuPro. In the final years before retirement, I was in international management and spent thousands of hours on airplanes to cities all over the world. While there were many disadvantages to that sort of lifestyle, there were also some rewards to it. First, I made acquaintances with some wonderful people I met and worked with; I hit my one hundredth country a month before I retired. Secondly, I accumulated hundreds of thousands of frequent flyer miles.

"Many of my former colleagues urged me to visit them after my retirement, and then I got a letter from the airline saying that my frequent flyer miles would expire unless I used them by the end of this year. So I decided to plan a trip around the world, not so much as a tourist, but to accomplish two purposes: to visit friends for perhaps the last time, and to try and do some good as a volunteer for The Rotary Foundation. I wondered if too much water had passed under the bridge for an old geezer like me to embark on such a trip. But then I read in *The Rotarian* magazine about Past Rotary International Director Charles Fogel who participated in a PolioPlus National Immunization Day in India at the age of 90, and 83-year-old Rotarian Wesley Rush from Illinois who volunteered for 10 days of NIDs in Central Africa. So I felt like a wimp for even considering not making the trip after that!

"My greatest challenge was where to go and what to include: The Rotary Foundation simply overwhelmed me with the number of projects they have going on simultaneously all over the world. This is my story, but more importantly, it is the story of how one ordinary fellow—just a regular Rotarian—became aware of the amazing work our Foundation is doing and in the tiniest way, how he was able to help make a difference in the world.

> "Don't die with your music still in you."
> – Dr. Wayne Dyer

"I headed west to spend a few days with my niece who married a Canadian and lives in New Westminster, British Columbia. I had not even planned that to be a part of my Rotary Foundation tour, but Debbie's next-door neighbor is a Rotarian and he invited me to attend his club meeting during my visit. As it happens, I got a foretaste of Rotary volunteerism. One of the club members, Dr. Irwin Stewart, is an otolaryngologist and a past district governor. Irwin traveled as a Rotary Volunteer to Uganda where he set up a large preventable-deafness project.[2] He applied that old maxim *give a man a fish, you feed him for a day; teach a man how to fish, and you feed him for a lifetime.* Dr. Stewart organized his program to teach local medical practitioners the latest diagnostic and treatment methods from the developed world.

"He returned time and again for five years, sometimes leading a team of up to 30 Rotarian and non-Rotarian volunteers on the long trip from Western Canada to Uganda to share their expertise with their African peers—and hundreds of truly grateful patients.

"I think we sometimes get so caught up in our business and social lives at home that we forget how much of a difference we can make in an area where the things we take for granted are but distant dreams. Let me share what Irwin Stewart's initiative and thoughtfulness led to:

- 24 health ministry surgeons were trained in how to perform modern temporal-bone ear microsurgery
- 100 education ministry staff members were taught to recognize deafness in children through audiometric testing
- 50 clinicians being able to recognize hearing loss and able to provide simple treatments
- Operating-room nurses were taught how to sterilize and set up microsurgical instruments

---

[2] As reported in *Rotary World*, April 2006

- Hospital technicians were trained to repair and maintain surgical equipment.

"It was one of the most interesting club programs I have ever seen. And here is what Dr. Stewart said: 'When those people reach the ability to train others, they are going to benefit the entire population of the country. What we have done is going to make a difference for the 2.6 million Ugandans with hearing problems.'

"As if that was not enough, Stewart's volunteers also provided 400 solar-powered hearing aids to deaf people who cannot benefit from surgery, equipped clinicians with basic diagnostic equipment, donated 250 used computers to schools for the deaf, and provided medical training materials, hospital and medical supplies, microscopes, textbooks... the list goes on and on!"

Duncan took a sip of water, and then clicked his remote control to advance the slide to show a map of the Pacific Ocean.

"I then flew southwest to the beautiful island nation of Fiji," he continued. "Just as with British Columbia, this was not meant to be part of my Rotary Foundation tour. I have an old family friend who serves in the diplomatic service, and he was assigned to Fiji. He has repeatedly urged me to visit him while he is there, so I thought I would use this trip as an opportunity to stop over for a few days.

"While I was there, I told Dave that the real purpose of my trip was to see Rotary in action. He told me about an amazing project that Rotarians—and The Rotary Foundation—were arranging in Fiji. Two days later, I found myself in the midst of it!

"Rotary clubs throughout the country sponsored the Fiji Health Festival,[3] in partnership with the Ministry of Health and a US$81,000 Matching Grant from The Rotary Foundation. They worked with Rotary clubs in Australia, New Zealand, and the USA in what seems to me to be an example of what President Frank has urged *us* to do: they shared their time, their talents, and their treasures. Many Rotarian health professionals traveled to Fiji as volunteers at treatment centers all over the country. They provided specialized medical treatment for patients with diabetes, dental-, and eye-, ear-, nose- and throat problems.

"Right alongside top ophthalmologists, dentists, and surgeons were local Rotarians and even Rotaract and Interact members. It was a wonderful world fellowship of people with different accents and skin colors and vocations—all working together to improve the lives of 3,600 people who came to the health festival.

"Last year, our club hosted our first GSE team— six really fine people from The Philippines. The team leader stayed in my home for a week, and we became good friends. When I told him of my idea to travel around the world, he insisted I visit him in Davao City and stay with his family. It was a very interesting city—one where Rotary is thriving.

"Johnny showed me a project his club operated, called Greenlife for Street Children.[4] Davao City has many orphaned and abandoned children. Hundreds of them run away from state orphanages—or are ejected when they reach their mid-teens, and then they face the harsh reality of survival on the streets. Many are forced into lives of crime, just to survive. Local Rotary

---

[3] As reported in *Rotary World*, April 2006
[4] As reported in *Rotary World*, April 2006

clubs began the Greenlife project to teach these kids job skills—after all, Vocational Service is one of our Four Avenues of Service. The Calgary Chinook Rotary Club contributed seed money, as did the host Waling-Waling Davao club. The Rotary Foundation then provided a Matching Grant.

"Johnny took me to a large field where the street kids were learning how to grow ornamental plants and commercial quantities of fresh vegetables. They had laid a water line for irrigation and were already reaping their first harvest and becoming self-sufficient. These were 60 of the poorest kids in the city; teenagers with no prospects, no hope for the future. And now, just a few weeks after their Rotary Foundation grant came through, they had useful skills, good jobs, a safe place to live, and were getting an education. However, the most important gift of all is that Rotary is giving them *hope*.

"Let's face it, none of us would ever have heard of these kids, or of Greenlife for Street Children—or probably even of Davao City. We would not have been able to respond to those needs because no matter how vital they are, they never would have made our TV news; they simply would have fallen below our radar screens. Yet I have seen these kids, and I have seen those not fortunate enough to be in Greenlife—and I give you my personal assurance: they need our help. Now, because of my contribution to The Rotary Foundation—*I can help!*"

Duncan stopped talking while clicking through five or six slides that showed teenage boys tending to rows of vegetables and lush-looking potted ornamental plants. Other pictures appeared on the screen of kids in school and of smiling, happy children linked arm in arm outside "Boystown Davao," their new home. Finally, the screen went blank, and then moved on to a map with a red line drawn from The Philippines to Thailand.

"My next stop was in the city of Chiang Mai, in northern Thailand," explained Duncan. "I should explain that I have a personal reason for selecting Chiang Mai. My nephew and his wife adopted a baby from Thailand; a beautiful little girl whose birth mother had left her family's impoverished home among the hill tribes near Chiang Rai. The recruiter told her parents that he would get her a job in a hotel in Chiang Mai, and gave the family an advance on her salary, but once in his custody, she became his indentured servant and he sold her into the sex trade. She was 13 at the time. The girl was held as a virtual prisoner, sometimes having to sleep with six or eight men a day in the sleazy brothels that tourists flock to in Chiang Mai. By 16, she was pregnant, and the daughter she delivered was taken from her so she could continue to earn money for her owners. When my nephew and his wife adopted Ashley, they tried to track down the birth mother to let her know that they would provide a lifetime of love for her baby girl, but they discovered the mother—now 17—had contracted AIDS, and before Ashley celebrated her first birthday, her mother was dead.

"This sort of thing is rampant in Thailand, particularly among ethnic minority hill-tribe people like Ashley's mother. It is human trafficking of the most despicable kind. However, right there in the city where Ashley was born and where her teenage mother endured so much pain and suffering, Rotary is now doing something to help.

"I visited the New Life Center, which is funded by The Rotary Foundation and individual clubs and districts in Japan, Thailand, and the USA. The Center serves as a safe haven for girls who have been—or who are at risk of being—exploited as sex workers or domestic slaves. There are 55 girls living in the New Life Center in Chiang Mai and another 36 in a second home near Chiang Rai, 200 kilometers to the north. The Center's professional staff provides an education; many of the girls are from nomadic tribes and speak only their indigenous language, so the program teaches them to read, write, and speak Thai. This dramatically improves their chances of finding a respectable job.

"The Center also provides counseling to help them overcome their abusive past, along with vocational training. Once again, The Rotary Foundation came through with Matching Grants: one to fund education, healthcare, and food costs for 40 girls for a year; the other to provide sewing machines and supplies to start a tailoring workshop. Yet another Rotary Foundation grant helped them establish a bakery.

"Fellow Rotarians, this is what you see on almost every street in Chiang Mai." Duncan paused while he showed a rapid succession of neon-lit go-go bars, striptease clubs, and shops with beautiful young women—girls, really—sitting on display, sometimes dressed in colorful long silk gowns, sometimes in mini-skirts. "They have numbers pinned on them," he said. "Numbers! These girls are as young as twelve, and have been plucked from their families far away and are now for sale by the hour to disgusting tourists or local businessmen looking for a good time. Almost none of these women will ever see the age of 30. Unless somebody helps them. And that is what you and I can do—today—through our Rotary Foundation.

"My nephew and his wife adopted Ashley with the thought of making it an open adoption. They planned to exchange freely photographs and letters with her birth mother as she grew up. However, that can never happen now, because she died before a place like the New Life Center could rescue her and offer her refuge and a safe future. I only pray that you and I can act in time to rescue the next group of girls before they are condemned to the same fate."

Duncan's voice cracked as he spoke his last words before looking back at the giant screen to cue the next slide. It showed a map of the world, with a red line extending from Thailand to East Africa.

"Actually, before we go to Africa, I just remembered an incident I would like to share with you," he said. "My flight from Chiang Mai to Nairobi required an overnight stay in Singapore. While awaiting my flight the next morning, I decided to have a coffee at the airport, and as I paid the cashier, the two men behind me noticed my Rotary pin. They introduced themselves as Rotarians from Denmark, so we sat and talked for about 15 minutes before they had to board their flight. They were *en route* to Bangladesh as Rotary Volunteers, working for a month to help solve a problem called Trachoma.

"Now, I must admit, I had never *heard* of Trachoma before meeting Hans and Erik. They explained that it is the leading infectious cause of preventable blindness in the world. The highest incidence of Trachoma cases is in communities with very poor sanitation and inadequate clean water, and half a *billion* people are at risk of infection, primarily in Asia and Africa. Apparently, the mother often contracts the bacterium and then passes it on to her children. Flies also transmit it by landing on the face of an infected person and then carrying it on to an uninfected person. According to the World Health Organization, 70 million people are now infected with Trachoma and two million are blind because of it. That one chance 15-minute meeting in

Singapore had quite an effect on me. Here were two ordinary folks from Denmark embarking on an unsung humanitarian mission to Bangladesh; it really drove home to me the realization of how our Foundation, and Rotary itself, is not an inanimate object; it is a living, breathing group of caring people who are passionate about their pledge of service to humanity. Danes and Canadians and Mexicans and Australians and Indians are literally crisscrossing the globe every hour of every day trying to bring real solutions to real problems— sometimes, solving problems that, as I admitted, we didn't even realize were there."

Duncan looked back at the screen as he brought up a slide showing his route, and then to another photograph of a group of men and women—the latter dressed in colorful dresses and headgear—building what looked like a dam.

"Welcome to Kenya!" he said, looking at his watch. "Oh dear, I see I am up against the clock. I am afraid they will give me the hook if I overstay my allotted time today, so this is going to be your tour of Africa: three countries in five minutes!

"My first stop on the continent was in Naivasha, a town in the arid Great Rift Valley region of Kenya. There were two water-related problems in Naivasha: first, there was no way of preserving the water from the rainy season to use when the drought returned. Second, the raw sewage from town seeped into the water supply and helped spread disease. Then Rotarians heard about the problem, and clubs in Kenya and The Netherlands began working on a solution. After consulting with the Westerveld Conservation Trust in Holland, they raised their own funds, along with a Rotary Foundation Matching Grant of almost US$10,000 and built a large dam. This created a retention pond that now holds enough water from the rainy season to serve the town all year long. Then they proceeded to introduce education programs and physical improvements to enhance the local hygiene conditions so that waste and drinking water are no longer mixed.

"They are so pleased with the results that they are now looking into underground water storage—and Dutch Rotarians, with Rotary Foundation help, are proposing similar projects in other drought-stricken areas of Kenya, Ethiopia, Tanzania, and Uganda."

Duncan took another sip of water and resumed his presentation. He seemed to be speaking faster now, perhaps aware of his time limit.

"I flew from Kenya to South Africa. About a year ago, I became interested in helping solve the dreadful scourge of HIV-AIDS, which as you all know is an epidemic in Africa. I had joined a Rotary Fellowship Group called Rotarians For Fighting AIDS. Then in 2006, Rotary International changed the name of some of these cause-related Rotary Fellowships to Rotary Action Groups. I like the name better, because the real purpose is for like-minded Rotarians to *take action* on problems, not just to have fellowship. Once again, this is an example of Rotary changing with the times.

"Anyway, one of our first steps was to start the African Network for Children Orphaned—ANCHOR— and we already won a US government grant of $8.1 million to improve the well-being of 146,000 orphans in six African countries. So I went to South Africa to attend a meeting of the Action Group.

"I wish I had time to tell you about the many ways Rotary is serving at-risk communities in Africa. Let me just touch on a few Rotarians who are at the tip of the iceberg.

"One is a man named Vic Bredenkamp, of the Rotary Club of Pietermaritzburg, South Africa. Vic was sort of a personal wake-up call to me, because he retired in 1991 after 30 years as a university professor—and *then* he went to work, this time, as an almost full-time Rotary volunteer. It is easy to do things for cute little babies and children, but Vic saw a need in some of the worst prisons in the country, and set about helping those whom it is sometimes hard to love.

"There are few places on earth more scary—or filled with more hopelessness and despair—than the insides of South Africa's overcrowded jails. Most of the inmates are poor, black, and illiterate. However, that did not deter Vic. He launched literacy and numeracy programs that taught prisoners what should be everybody's basic human right: how to read and write. First one club member and then another and then another nervously accompanied Vic to the prison—and were so heartened by the gratitude their students showed that they kept going back.

"He expanded the program to other prisons in other cities, and The Rotary Foundation gave a grant to buy some of the teaching materials. Today, hundreds—yes, my friends, *hundreds*—of once-illiterate men and women can now read, write, and understand math. They can exchange letters with their families for the first time, and as some of them earn their freedom, they are more likely to have the skills and self esteem necessary to hold jobs and stay out of trouble in the future. I think it was best summed up by the headline I read in a newspaper: 'For many in Pietermaritzburg's New Prison the three R's no longer mean raping, robbing, and rioting, thanks to a new literacy programme undertaken by Rotary!'

"I love Africa. I traveled there many times for my employer. It has so many problems—and so much potential. Africa needs our help, and that is what is so powerful about real Rotarians. They look beyond the borders that separate people, like skin color and religion and politics—and they say, 'How can we help?'

"For sure, Africa has a long way to go, but because of people like you, a child whose name you do not need to know will never be crippled from polio. He will not die from malaria because he will sleep tonight under a mosquito net provided by Rotarians. He will not have to miss school tomorrow to walk five miles each way to carry water from the closest well—because his mother can now draw safe clean drinking water from the well installed with a Rotary Foundation grant. And when he grows up, he can apply for a Rotary Foundation scholarship to travel to the developed world where he can learn—and take home—solutions to assure that the next generation from his village will learn only from history books about the problems so prevalent there today."

> "If you want to run fast, run alone; if you want to run far, run together."
> African proverb

Duncan glanced at his watch and winced. He looked over to the sergeant at arms, who was now standing at stage left—a sure sign that Duncan should end his presentation.

"I am afraid I don't have the time to tell you about the Rotarians of Taiwan who are providing for the education of 1,000 needy children in Gambia. I only wish I could show you the slides of the old military barracks in Namibia that Rotary clubs in Germany and Namibia have converted into a school, orphanage, and hospital. Moreover, we did not even get to South America, where I wanted to tell you about the Rotary Foundation Matching Grant that helped Rotarians build one hundred low-cost shelters for impoverished homeless families in Curitiba, Brazil.

"And perhaps that is the way I *should* end my presentation. For no single speaker, indeed, no weekend conference nor even an entire book could possibly tell the story of The Rotary Foundation. Our story has too many chapters, too many actors, too many heroes to be summed up this way. It once was said that the sun never sets on the British Empire. Rotary has no empire, but the sun never sets on the projects and programs and people at work for The Rotary Foundation.

"I close with the greeting I learned in Africa: *Mutende abanandi:* 'Peace to you, my friends.'"

"In the days and weeks after the devastating tsunami in South Asia, Rotarians came from all around the world to help. They came and were able to get to work immediately because they joined their follow Rotarians who lived where the tsunami had struck, people who knew exactly what the needs were and how best to meet them and who were able to bypass local governments. Unlike the other aid workers, who stayed in distant hotels and flew into the affected areas every morning, the Rotarians stayed with the people. Today, the television cameras are gone, but Rotary is still there."

– William B. Boyd,
2006-2007 President,
Rotary International, at the
2006 International Assembly.

## CHAPTER 9

# They Get It!

I glanced down at the outline of my final remarks as I heard the District Governor-Elect introduce me to the packed ballroom. The effects of my long international flight just 48 hours earlier had now hit me with full force—and I had a five o'clock wake-up call for a flight to Osaka, Japan, in the morning. Yet I could not allow any sign of being tired. This had been a wonderful conference. The organizers had filled every session with dynamic, inspiring, educational presenters—and enthusiastic audiences. Now it was up to me to close the conference with a message that was at once motivational—but with the lasting impact of stirring inside these Rotarians *real* action, both in their physical and financial support of The Rotary Foundation.

"... so ladies and gentlemen, please join me one last time in welcoming Frank Devlyn." I walked to the lectern, gesturing for the audiences to take their seats.

"My family of Rotary, I was just sitting there wondering how I should deliver my message," I began, in complete honesty. "You expect, I suppose, a past president of Rotary International to give you a speech that is informative. But the encyclopedia is filled with *information*, and I suspect most of you would fall asleep if I just relayed information to you for the next thirty minutes. Others might counsel me to give a motivational speech, and yet we have all experienced motivational speakers who pump up their audiences with jokes and inspiring anecdotes—but a week later, there is nothing left, because the speech was all fluff and no substance. The effect of most motivational speakers is ephemeral and the air soon is all gone from the balloon.

"The Rotary Foundation is too important for that to happen. You all came here to this conference because you cared enough to want to take our Foundation to new heights. My job—and yours—is to make sure, to make the absolute commitment right now—that we *will* leave this place and become true ambassadors for The Rotary Foundation: in our clubs, our districts, our communities, and in our personal lives.

"Do I have your pledge to treat the matter that seriously?" I stopped and looked out into the audience. What sounded like several hundred voices responded, "Yes!"

"Yesterday, I spoke of Arch Klumph, founder of The Rotary Foundation. Even before Rotary International had officially approved the establishment of the Foundation, Arch Klumph wrote in 1917 that there are some people, quote, *who are seeking ways and means of leaving some part of their wealth where it may do the greater good for humanity. What better-equipped organization than Rotary International can be found to be entrusted with such funds?* unquote.

"I have made my theme, as Chairman of the Trustees, *Leaving a Legacy*, and several speakers in the last two days have continued to stress a similar thread. It is almost as if we had all compared notes before the conference—but we did not. Let me pose a philosophical question here: why is it important to human beings that they need to leave a legacy? Do we really want to live forever?

"Since the earliest times, people have sought such a promise, In the Middle Ages, we saw origins of the fable of the Fountain of Youth. Ponce de Leon and Christopher Columbus even sailed across the Atlantic in vain searches of it. The legend has lasted for centuries—and some still seek it.

"In February 2006, as Chairman of The Rotary Foundation's Board of Trustees, I addressed all incoming district governors in the world when they attended the International Assembly in San Diego, California. I told them, 'Living forever in the physical sense is not possible. However, to leave a legacy that lasts in perpetuity might just be the next best thing. The Rotary Foundation's Permanent Fund enables Rotarians to create their own legacy to do good in the world forever.'

"How big would it be if every Rotarian on earth gave $100 a year to the Permanent Fund? We would build a core fund with a *billion* dollars in assets by 2025, and would be able to pay for massive global humanitarian projects the size of PolioPlus—in cash—on a regular basis.

"And what if you gave another hundred dollars every year to our Foundation's Annual Fund? I was just in Venice and tourists were standing in line to pay one hundred dollars for 40-minute gondola rides up a smelly canal. I visited a glass factory and they were selling a set of glass sea turtles for $40,000. *Forty thousand dollars!* Now please do not misunderstand me: I am not against the memorable experience of taking a gondola ride, and neither do I hate sea turtles. However, it strikes me that some people—including some Rotarians—would think nothing of spending money on such trivialities, and then give nothing at all on an annual basis to our Foundation. You see, there are some people in our communities, our workplaces, and sadly, even in our Rotary clubs, who hear the stories and see the pictures of the work The Rotary Foundation is doing to make a real difference in the world—but who just don't get it.

"Today, I want to tell you about the others; about those who *do* get it. The people who say that for as much fun as they might get from a gondola ride, they also know their hundred-dollar gift to The Rotary Foundation will restore the sight to three people. They get it because their legacy is to give three blind people the opportunity to see their children and to hold a job, and to provide for their families. The people who get it know that their one hundred dollars will buy 10 mosquito nets to protect 20-30 people from malaria, or will provide safe drinking water for ten families.

"But there I go again! You see, every time I get excited about The Rotary Foundation, I end up citing statistics. I tell people about the 22,000 Matching Grants in 166 countries and the 52,000 individuals from 12,000 GSE teams The Rotary Foundation has made possible—not to mention the two *billion* children we have saved from polio. However, The Rotary Foundation is not about statistics. It is about saving lives, and about improving our world, and about bringing together people of differing ethnic and cultural backgrounds to achieve the goal of peace in the world.

"Remember, we *became* an organization because Paul Harris brought four people from different backgrounds together in the spirit of fellowship, and soon afterwards we developed the concept that makes us stand out worldwide. We believe in—and we actively practice—service not to ourselves, but to people in need around the planet.

"As I mentioned yesterday, we do that by sharing our Four T's: our thinking, our talents, our time, and our treasures. As we began Rotary's second century of service to humankind, I began asking Rotarians who were on the front line of sharing their Four T's—the people who *get* it—exactly *why* they do so. After all, if I am going to persuade somebody to embark on a journey to a place to which they have never been, doesn't it make sense to ask a person who has already made the trip *why* they went there and what they liked about it?

"Bill Boyd, Rotary International's President in 2006-2007, says this: 'We won't *sell* The Rotary Foundation until we can tell stories of what it does.' That is good advice for me—in my talk to you today. And it is excellent advice for you, as you carry the message back to your clubs. Bill says 'We give best when our emotions are touched by things that happen. Looking at numbers is sterile. We do not get emotionally involved with numbers. But we also don't need to go very far to touch people's emotions.'

"So how do we connect with our friends back in Rotary—and in the greater community at home? I believe the best way is through being involved. At the lowest level, that means we should be constantly involved with the work our Foundation is doing, through the Web site, articles in *The Rotarian* magazine, and from people who serve in the field. We should communicate these inspiring events with our friends in weekly Rotary Foundation moments at our club meetings and in the bulletin. Look what Sue did: her club went from lowest in the district in Rotary Foundation *per capita* giving to the highest—in a single year—after she communicated with the members every week and conveyed to the members a sense of pride and ownership in their Foundation.

"The far end of this involvement continuum would be the recruitment of fellow Rotarians and friends to participate in the field to work as Rotary Foundation volunteers. It also means making a personal commitment to sharing our resources with the Foundation as significant contributors.

"I say this with some hesitation, because I know I had your full attention until I mentioned the words *make a significant financial contribution*. Then I saw several of you looking around nervously, hoping that I was speaking to the *other* people in the room.

"But I wasn't. I was talking to you. To each one of you. I know it is uncomfortable to ask people to give money—especially when we ask them to step out of their comfort zone and make a *significant* gift. However, it is *our* responsibility to do just that. It is our duty to set an example by giving ourselves, and it is our duty to leverage that gift by recruiting others to do the same. That is all part of the legacy we will leave.

"I have been richly blessed not only to have a wonderful family but also to have a successful business career. That has enabled me to give back to humankind through Rotary, and as I have criss-crossed the world as a Rotary International director, and then president, and later as Rotary Foundation Chairman, I have been deeply touched by the real people who are serving real people in what the first President Bush called 'A thousand points of light.'

"I think of people like Zoe Craig, who in 2003-2004 served as a Rotary Foundation Ambassadorial Scholar in Chile. Ordinary Rotarians in the Rotary Club of Albuquerque, New Mexico sponsored her Master's-level studies in International Law in Conflict and Peace Studies, and she decided to spend some of her free time in Santiago, Chile volunteering at an orphanage and teaching English to low-income college students. Zoe personified the maxim 'think globally while acting locally.' She helped construct affordable housing for poor families near Santiago and is working with the Rotary Clubs of Albuquerque to get a Matching Grant for a microcredit program that will allow impoverished Chilean women to become small-business owners.

You see, my Rotary friends, everyone we meet would say, 'I care about the poor, the hungry, the diseased,' and so on. However, *real* Rotarians go beyond *caring*; they care enough to *act*.

"I remember D. K. Lee, a Past Rotary International Director, and Trustee of The Rotary Foundation telling me that one Korean Rotarian donated $250,000 to the Foundation because he felt our Rotary Peace Scholars might one day help reunite his country. On another occasion, I met with Rotarians in Taipei, Taiwan, and 106 of them each gave $10,000 to The Rotary Foundation. Why would they do that, you might wonder. Perhaps the best answer came from Paul Elder of Pittsburgh, who made a gift to our Foundation of $7.5 million—the largest single gift any person has ever made. And this is what Paul said: 'The Rotary Foundation can do more good with my money than anyone else.' His gift—and yours—will continue to provide help for years to come.

"David and Lis Ker, of the Rotary Club of Vancouver South, Canada, met a visiting Russian professor back in 1993. When the Kers enquired how they could help with Russia's transition to democracy, Professor Polischuk advised them to go there and teach—adding that Russians had not smiled for 70 years. Six months later, the Kers were on their way to Novosibirsk, Siberia for a seven-week teaching assignment as Rotary volunteers. While there, they built numerous and deep-seated relationships and helped charter the Rotary Club of Novosibirsk. Two years later, they returned to help charter the Rotary Club of Barnaul.

"They got their home club and district involved, and this led to 20 Russian Rotarians and spouses participating in a friendship and training visit to Rotary clubs in District 5040, British Columbia, Canada. The Kers went on to donate CA $50,000 a year for the next ten years, endowing Rotary Foundation scholarships to bring university students from Siberia to British Columbia—their legacy to the Russian clubs they helped to form. Think about that: just two decades ago two countries stared at each other across the frozen Arctic as enemies and now they are joined in helping the next generation succeed with a world-class education and training in ethics, peacemaking, and job skills that will benefit *both* communities for years to come. And all of this because *one* Rotarian cared—and cared enough to act. The Kers made a significant gift because of their own hands-on contact with people in another country—people who touched their hearts. Yet we do not *have to* physically take potential donors abroad to inspire them to give to The Rotary Foundation.

"John Brodbeck is a long-time Rotarian who had the desire and ability to give to our Foundation—but nobody ever asked him to do so. Those of you who are club and district Rotary Foundation chairs, listen to what John told me: 'No one ever asked Marilee and me to consider giving a large sum to our Foundation. Little did my fellow Rotarians know that for many years I had dreamed of making a larger donation to the Permanent Fund so that I might continue to be a Rotarian long after I leave this life. In hindsight, I am sure most of my fellow Rotarians thought I was lucky to become a Paul Harris Fellow and didn't want to embarrass me by asking for a larger donation.'

"My friends, Rotary today is full of members who give a thousand dollars to The Rotary Foundation to become a Paul Harris Fellow, and then tens of thousands—or millions—to their universities, or other charities with which they have only a relatively minor acquaintance compared to their weekly involvement in Rotary. And why does that happen? It is because those charities ask for the gift—and we are too scared or too embarrassed or too untrained to do so. We have an incredible, amazing, unmatchable story to tell; we should not hide our light under a bushel."

I hesitated to take a sip of water while looking at the audience. Was I connecting with them or was I turning them off? I would not know until long after I left the city and compared Rotary Foundation giving for these four districts over the next three or four years. I knew from personal experience that most people do not like to be asked—or to ask—for money, and yet that was exactly what I was seeking of them. A few heads had nodded, but that was not necessarily a sign that they would put action behind the agreement. I thought back to the start of my own giving cycle to The Rotary Foundation and realized that I made my first donation more out of one-upmanship than from true benevolence. I saw two other members in my district give a thousand dollars each to become Paul Harris Fellows and thought "I want to be just like them." Hardly the best example of altruism, and yet, as I later learned more about how my small donation was helping, the more I wanted to give. Rotary communicated to me the problems that existed in our world; The Rotary Foundation gave me the opportunity to be a part of the solution.

"So what is the key?" I wondered aloud to the audience. "Why would somebody give ten thousand dollars to an animal charity, or a million dollars to build a school gymnasium? Understand, I am not criticizing animal charities or your alma maters! Far from it! I am admiring them, because they were able to make the emotional connection between the donor and their own need—and then made the case why *they* should be ideal recipients of a portion of the donor's resources. Personally, I look upon Rotary with more love than I do the universities where I received my education, and I think many of you feel the same way. Now, do you not think The Rotary Foundation—*our* Rotary Foundation—is a worthy beneficiary? Why did people name a library with their ten-million-dollar gift to the school? So their name would live on long after they passed from this earth. *They left a legacy.*

> "In Thailand, [Lorna and I] saw an informal education center in a library that had been flooded in the tsunami and is now refurbished. The center is training young people in computer skills, using its 10 modern computers—the ones that Rotary gave. In the Philippines, in a city where there had never been a school to serve the needs of autistic children, I saw the school that stands there today—the one that Rotary built."
> – William B. Boyd, 2006-2007 President, Rotary International

"Remember John Brodbeck—who was never asked to give? Only after he became a past district governor and *knew about* the work of The Rotary Foundation did his perspective change. He was asking Rotarians to support the Foundation and it struck him that he really should set an example by making his own commitment to the cause he was promoting to others. The more he looked into it, the more compelled he and Marilee felt about becoming Major Donors—which they did, at the Level Six category, but even this was a decision that took two years to evolve. John said this proves you should not ask once and then stop, adding that he and Marilee became Major Donors so that he might continue to be a Rotarian long after he leaves this life. He told me, 'Too many Rotarians think once they have become a Paul Harris Fellow they will automatically go to Rotary Heaven and that they have done their part to make the world a better place. I don't think so! The Rotarians who became Paul Harris Fellows four or more years ago need to be thanked for their past efforts, but we need to ask, *what about the person who desperately needs our help today?* What about the children of the world who are dying because they do not have food, water, or shelter? Do you just say 'sorry' and forget about them? The Rotarians' contributions made over three years ago are long gone, spent, and not able to help anyone either today or in the future.'

"I should explain that John Brodbeck is not a rich man. He was a child of the Great Depression whose father died when he was three and who grew up in a house with nine people. He told me the family was poor, but thankfully, he was not smart enough to know it! His enduring memories to this day are of friends and neighbors who helped his family through their difficult times. Today, as a Rotarian, he is simply passing on that same gift of caring and sharing with people in our global village who are suffering through times of hardship, poverty, and disease. The Rotary Foundation—*his* Rotary Foundation—gives him the ability to do that, to leave his legacy.

"Not only is our Rotary Foundation working around the clock in countless sites worldwide, we are also leveraging our ability to help by partnering with other humanitarian organizations that already have experience and infrastructure in areas new to us. Let me tell you about Un Sophal.[5] Sophal had both legs ripped from his body when he stepped on a land mine in Cambodia. After six months in the hospital, the authorities discharged him—condemning the teenager to a lifetime as a beggar, an outcast in one of the world's most desperate countries. Then Sophal heard about the Kien Khleang Physical Rehabilitation Center in Pnomh Penh—a project operated by the Vietnam Veterans of America Foundation. Several Rotary Clubs and your Rotary Foundation support the Kien Khleang Center, and they not only provided Sophal with prosthetic legs and a wheel chair, they gave him a job as a technician making wheelchairs and prostheses for other land mine victims. Now 35, Sophal is married, mobile, and can provide for his four children—and give hope to the many of the 40,000 other land mine victims who live in Cambodia. You see, my Rotary Foundation is now Un Sophal's foundation, too.

"How can you give your Four T's: your thinking, your talent, your time, and your treasure to give new legs to more people like Sophal? *That*, my family of Rotary, is the question I leave you with today; the question I challenge you to answer. I talked this afternoon about major donors and million-dollar gifts, but do not let that distract you. If just one of you here today thinks 'The Rotary Foundation is out of my league because I could never afford to make such a large contribution,' then I have failed in my mission this

---

[5] as reported in *The Rotarian*, August 2005, p.38

weekend. If you *can* give thousands, or know somebody can—that is wonderful. However, I would much rather get a commitment from everybody that you will each give *something* every year than to be caught up on specific amounts from one or two people.

"In my year as your international president, I chose as my theme, *Create Awareness and Take Action.* That was in 2000 and 2001, and yet it is as appropriate and as vital for us to use as a motto as you leave this conference today. I tried to create awareness of our incredible 90-year commitment to humankind through our Foundation with my opening presentation on one extraordinary life—The Rotary Foundation's founder, Arch Klumph. Sue took action in her year as club president by focusing on the work of the Foundation at every meeting for 52 weeks. Bob created awareness and demonstrated that when he took action—immunizing children from polio and volunteering in the Jaipur Limb Camp he became an energized Rotarian. Duncan could have used his retirement playing golf or fishing, but he took action and traveled around the world as a Rotary volunteer—and he told us *he* was the one who felt the most rewarded from the experience.

"Family of Rotary, the presenters of this conference have created an awareness that cannot—must not—be ignored. You are aware of how your Rotary Foundation gives life to babies at risk from polio. You are aware of Rotary's growing core of specially trained ambassadors of peace and conflict resolution. You are aware of how our Rotary Foundation is making the promise of safe drinking water a reality in villages on three continents. You are aware of projects promoting literacy, self-sufficiency, and restoring sight to the blind. You are aware of how Rotarians in Ohio are helping land mine victims in Cambodia, and how our

Korean colleagues are providing *pro bono* surgery in Bangladesh, and how Australian Rotarians are helping the new democracy in East Timor build a nation free of oppression and corruption.

"My fellow Rotarians, as you get into your cars to drive home, I ask you *not* to turn on your mobile phones and car radios. My final request is for you to use that time of tranquility free from distractions. We have created awareness of your Rotary Foundation, *my* Rotary Foundation, *OUR* Rotary Foundation. Now it is up to *you* to take action—*to get it*. The needs are great. The cause is unbeatable. The time is now.

*Viva Rotary!*

*Viva our Rotary Foundation!*

*Muchas Gracias!*"

"I am amazed at what Rotary can do internationally. In March 2002, while I was the President of my club, I had one of my most important experiences because in my country there was no insulin, for both poor and rich people and I wrote to Rotarians of District 1220 in the U.K. And then occurred once more the miracle of the Rotarian friendship: only seventeen days after I wrote my e-mail, we got all the insulin that San Juan Province needed for a complete month."

– Norma Beatrice Kalejman, Argentina.

## AFTERWORD

# Where to From Here?

**By Luis Giay, President of
Rotary International 1996-1997,
Chairman, The Rotary Foundation
Board of Trustees 2006-2007**

I would like to share with you an exciting subject that is going to be a real challenge for you as well as for me: a future vision for The Rotary Foundation. If we talk about a vision for the future, we need to recognize that we live just as much in an age of unprecedented need as of unprecedented promise. The possibilities for "doing good in the world" have never been greater.

Our Rotary Foundation is changing and adapting as never before. Rotary's success in its second century depends on our having a strong, energetic, international, flexible, competent, organized, visionary Foundation, one that is able to respond to the world's needs and especially to the needs of Rotarians and their clubs. Everything we need to change the world is within our grasp. We need vision and visionaries!

Allow me now to share with you the primary objective of The Rotary Foundation Trustees with respect to the future:

1.  Our goal is to have a premier Foundation that is ready to help and serve Rotary International, clubs, and Rotarians and which enables them to offer service projects of greater significance to their communities.

2.  We want a cutting-edge, forward-looking Foundation, equipped to take proactive, rather than reactive, steps to solve problems, a Foundation that is ready to support Rotary in its second century with determination and fortitude.

3.  Our Foundation should be ready to serve Rotarians without piling more work, more paper, more bureaucracy on them. We want to give Rotarians immediate solutions right away—today, if possible!

4.  We also want a Foundation that will get Rotarians much more involved in the administration of projects at the district level and will facilitate the process of project approval, delivery of project funds, and the submission of final reports.

5.  Our Foundation must have the appropriate tools, structure, and capacity to face the problems of the future. Our Foundation needs people of vision who will anticipate potential challenges so that our resources may be optimally effective for everyone.

6.  There will be much discussion by 2007 regarding programs to succeed PolioPlus. I am confident that when polio is eradicated, Rotarians will be eager to take on a new challenge.

7.  We want a financially solid Foundation with a Permanent Fund able to invest more than $400 million in programs annually by 2015. That's

almost equivalent to a PolioPlus program every two years!

8. It is essential that we have a trustworthy, consistent Foundation that exercises careful stewardship of its funds. Tomorrow's Foundation will enjoy the same prestige it does today; it will be a premier Foundation for our donors.

9. Our Foundation should become a top option as a charitable entity for the great majority of Rotarians. The Rotary Foundation will have to decide whether to take an active stand on a trend that will become reality over the next 25 years: $300 trillion will change hands and pass from one generation to another as older people die. A large portion of these resources will be transferred to foundations, charitable agencies, churches, nonprofit organizations, etc. Should our Rotary Foundation continue in a passive role as this phenomenon unfolds? *No!* Our Rotary Foundation must have a well-defined, aggressive policy in place for receiving additional contributions.

10. Our Foundation will form strong alliances for service, secure financial partners to carry out projects with real impact, and take on new corporate projects just as successful as PolioPlus. In sum, our Foundation will be one that will make us increasingly proud of being Rotarians.

This truly international committee has consulted several experts, surveyed over 20,000 Rotarians, and collected more significant opinions, background material, and publications than had ever been done in our Foundation's history.

This, then, is the Future Vision Plan for The Rotary Foundation:

1. We will have to consolidate programs into four major areas: health, education, environment, and world peace. If you think carefully about all of our current programs, you will see that they ultimately fall under one of these general headings.

2. We must have the good sense *not to create more programs* but concentrate instead on supporting and funding Rotarians' service activities. I think we should simplify The Rotary Foundation as much as possible because people lose interest in an ongoing program if it becomes the domain of a group of experts.

3. New programs, what I call "megaprograms," will appear. Today's Rotary Foundation is itself a megaprogram of Rotary International. The new megaprograms will have a particular trait: Everyone can participate and millions can receive the benefits. An unbeatable formula!

4. Humanitarian programs will be the superstar of The Rotary Foundation's future. By 2010, humanitarian programs will represent close to 90 percent of our overall program budget. The Foundation will have a decidedly humanitarian profile, and this will be one of the most significant conceptual changes in Rotary's history.

5. But there is a problem: How much money will we need to keep up these activities? Our Foundation's funding needs will grow by at least 10 percent every year. In 2007, we will need $150 million and, by 2010, $200 million, and these are annual figures. Can we even imagine a Foundation of such scope?

6. Now, imagine a Foundation with a Permanent Fund in excess of a billion dollars financing pro-

grams costing more than $250 million dollars per year. Is this a utopian vision? *No!* It will be a reality before we know!

7. So, we will have to make appropriate plans for another historic moment in the area of finance, a time when the Permanent Fund can support all the Foundation's annual programs and we can phase out undesignated contributions. In other words, the "Permanent Megafund" will be the driving force that will ensure the survival and continuity of The Rotary Foundation and Rotary International.

8. The time will have come for new strategic alliances, and I have a sense of the shape they will take. But regardless of whether we join with governments, NGOs (nongovernmental organizations), or others, we will need to be ready to step in at the right moment.

*A Paul Harris Fellow is a person who is been recognized through the gift of $1,000 or more to The Rotary Foundation. The Paul Harris Fellow recognition program was started in 1957 to express the Foundation's appreciation for substantial contributions to what was then the Foundation's only program: international scholarships. The $1,000 level remains the same a half-century later.*

*The first Paul Harris Fellow was Allison G. Brush, past Rotary International Director from Laurel, Mississippi, USA. Rufus F. Chapin, past Rotary International Treasurer and an original 1905 member of Rotary Club of Chicago, was the second Paul Harris Fellow. A total of 12 Paul Harris Fellows were recognized that first year.*

*In 2006, The Rotary Foundation named the one-millionth Paul Harris Fellow.*

9. I envision an increasingly important role for Rotary International and The Rotary Foundation in preserving peace. The Rotary Centers for International Studies, a Rotary university for peace, a large corps of volunteers, the urban peace options—in short, a more than fascinating challenge to keep order, justice, and peace throughout the world.

10. One thing of which I am convinced, though, is that we must organize ourselves so that Rotary International and The Rotary Foundation can act within a national framework without losing their international character. Clearly, in every community, we will need to cooperate with the "third sector" that involves neither government authorities nor corporate entities. We can imagine the picture: thousands of volunteers out in the field, engaged in a rather simple activity. While governments use public funds for private ends, volunteers make use of private funds to serve the public good, filling the gaps that even governments are unable to address.

By now you probably can't wait to ask, "Luis, all these future challenges, changes, and innovations that you are describing —will our Rotary Foundation be ready to deal with them when the time comes?" I am sure that already now, right here today, we have the ability to stand up to them and come out ahead. Why do I feel this way?

My message is one of great optimism, a highly positive note. We are the guardians of our Rotary Foundation, and we have made good use up to the present of this wonderful tool. But the Foundation is also a bridge reaching across to the future, a bridge on which we may safely tread. Plans for the future of

Rotary will travel along the road of hope that is The Rotary Foundation.

Some of you may say that I have been too much of an idealist in this presentation. But I know that I stand before many idealists to whom these words of the Argentinean philosopher José Ingenieros well apply: "Only those who have the will to fight for a better world while living in an imperfect one deserve to be called idealists."

I want to encourage you to continue working and supporting our Foundation because the challenges for Rotary in its next century will only be another test for us to pass so that

The voice of every Rotarian may resound

Proclaiming the ideal of service,

For the most noble gesture in the world

Is to help one another by sharing the gift of a better life.

We will *Lead the Way* with our Rotary Foundation!

(Excerpted from his speech to incoming district governors at the 2006 International assembly, San Diego, California, USA)

A visionary Rotary Foundation Matching Grant project, carried out by Czech and German Rotary clubs, has improved life for older people and the disabled of all ages in West Bohemia, Czech Republic.

"Many of the old, poor, and handicapped remain forgotten, even after the Iron Curtain breakdown," said Horst Melzer, past governor of District 1880 (Germany) and Dobroslav Zemen, past governor of District 2240 (Czech Republic and Slovakia). "Unfortunately, they have missed the opportunity to adapt themselves to the free world."

One German and one Czech Rotary club teamed up to carry out each component of the four-fold project. The effort provided rehabilitation and training equipment for mentally disabled children in a social care institute; beds for handicapped seniors in a long-term care facility; a minibus to transport children with multifunctional handicaps to and from a special education school; and a minibus to take mentally disabled clients to and from therapeutic workshops.

# Appendix A

# Why Me?

### Personal testimonies from Rotarians
### who have made significant gifts to
### The Rotary Foundation

\* \* \* \* \*

During the period of my life as a 'young adult,' my major time and effort was spent in Boy Scout activities. They taught me to be helpful to those in need, perform service to others, and respect the diversities of the people around me. I attended a Boy Scout camp one summer when we experienced a polio epidemic. It killed two boys and paralyzed six more. Over 1,000 boys were sent home and quarantined for the rest of the summer. I was among the lucky ones that was not affected and had no idea what caused this terrible plague. I vowed that some day I hoped I could prevent others from getting polio. Rotary gave me that chance in 1979.

That year I was District Governor and the Health, Hunger, and Humanity program of The Rotary Foundation gave its first polio vaccine grant to The Philippines to immunize one million children. By 1985, Rotary's PolioPlus program, together with the Pan American Health Organization, visualized a polio-free world and Rotary, with its partners WHO, UNICEF, and CDC continued to play a central role in global efforts to eradicate polio.

When the first PolioPlus Campaign was created to raise $120 million, I had just retired and agreed to volunteer for two years as the International Executive Coordinator to help organize and train Rotarians worldwide. My travels took me to 30 countries and exposed me to health authorities, where I learned that immunizations in the United States were worse than many of the developing countries.

**Your gift of $100 can:**

- Buy tuition and books for one year of school for two children in Kenya.
- $500 can buy a ten-month food supply for a child in Guatemala
- $1,000 can pay for clean drinking water for over 300 people in India.

Vaccine-preventable infectious diseases remain killers on a huge scale worldwide. Through travel and immigration, these diseases can easily reenter the U.S. population if residents become complacent and forego immunizations. This applies to newborns through senior citizens that, in all likelihood, have not been educated on the importance of immunizations.

My wife and I felt that Rotary Clubs in the U.S., working within their communities, could partner with local health authorities, schools, religious institutions, service organizations, and others to address the needs of underserved people of all ages. These Grants provide up to $1,000 in matching funds to U.S. Rotary clubs to help them achieve the greatest vaccine needs in their own community. After five years of experience, almost 350 Grants have been issued in 46 U.S. states and most Rotary clubs continue their activities after the grant has been completed.

Only through an organization like The Rotary Foundation could a program like this be successful. The Rotary Foundation efficiently processes the necessary funding in a professional manner, applying ethical standards internationally. Its unquestioned reliability gives confidence to all the partners, who are proud to be associated with such an outstanding organization. From a personal standpoint, it gave us great satisfaction that our investment would be put to good use and made us proud to be associated with all levels of the program.

– Jack B. Blane,
Past District Governor,
District 6440

\* \* \* \* \*

I feel that people have to be motivated to give. With Po-lioPlus, it was my desire for my children and grandchildren to not live with the same fear of Polio as I did.

Thereafter, it was seeing living conditions in India and the Philippines first hand that motivated me to want to help. This was spurred on by meeting a Rotarian in India who in 1987 was giving half his income every week towards his club's projects (he now gives all his income and they live off his wife's earnings). When I commented to him that he made me feel humble, he replied, "When I go outside my front door every morning it is right there in front of me. I cannot escape it." Then he asked: "What do you see when you step outside your front door every morning?" That hit me right between the eyes and I just wanted to help this guy as much as I could.

We need to encourage Rotarians from developed countries to visit their brothers and sisters in the developing countries.

– **Ken Collins,**
**Past Director of Rotary International,**
**Past Trustee of The Rotary Foundation**

\* \* \* \* \*

Over the past 20 or so years, I asked many Rotary leaders to give me their reasons for their continued support of Rotary and especially our Foundation. I continue to learn from these testimonials. I asked the first Permanent Fund National Advisors at their initial training back in 1995, "Why is the Permanent Fund important to you?" Most of these 28 PDGs responded by saying it would help make a difference in the world. A poem that I once read motivates me to continue to lead when possible and ask for money for The Rotary Foundation. I hope the poem serves as my legacy to my family and friends:

God has given me a place on earth
to be here for a while

I hope that as I'm passing through
I'll make somebody smile.

I want to make life easier for
all those that I meet

I ask God for His blessings to the
strangers on the street.

I hope I'll never fail a child if
I can help somehow.

I want to be as generous as
my resources allow

And when my life on earth is done,
it will be my final plea:

Let someone, somewhere think or say:
"You made a difference to me."

– Lou Piconi, Vice President
Rotary International 2000-2001

\* \* \* \* \*

I would like to answer why my wife and I have elected to endow a Peace Scholarship in The Rotary Foundation in addition to being major donors.

While Elaine and I were formalizing our trusts, we sat down to consider where we could direct our bequests. Obviously, we first considered our children. But then we considered those areas that had been of personal interest and areas of continuing involvement in our lives. We first considered the church, then religious and character forming organizations, our universities as well as Rotary International and its Foundation. As mentioned before, we had supported each of these areas with our personal time, efforts, and funds. We thought we knew the strengths of each enterprise.

As we considered the leadership pool, the constant monitoring, the breadth of exposure, the acceptance of the organization and the efficiency of reaction, we selected Rotary. During the period of leadership in the Polio Campaign, I saw us literally touch everyone in the world. I could see that wherever there was freedom, there was Rotary. Government officials opened their doors to Rotary. Kings and presidents listened to our messages. Leaders of business, the UN, UNICEF, World Bank, CDC, and WHO all responded to our calls for aid and then became almost friends. They respected our leadership standards from the club to the international levels.

Rotary has reached a point at which it is poised not only to resolve the war against polio but also to serve as a world peacemaker against hunger, illiteracy, and shortages of fresh water. We have become a private peacemaker working with the world's public institutions. The future is so rich for our unselfish assistance to resolve these problems. One of the most exciting areas for me was the addition of Peace Scholarships for 70 people annually. The effort to bring together competent leaders and to train them in conflict resolution and international customs allowed us to see a bright future for resolution of conflicts. Incidents such as border disputes have been resolved by Rotarians and the UN Charter was created with Rotarian assistance. Those two examples are just a beginning of what is possible when peace-loving competent worldwide leaders negotiate in the future.

The potential is boundless. The leadership of our organization is superior, is filled with fresh ideas, provides constant surveillance and outstanding stewardship, and possesses an infrastructure like no other organization in the world.

I am betting that if an answer to suffering and hardship of all kinds is found, it will be by a private organization like Rotary. So I ask, "Why not Rotary?" We are comfortable with our choice.

**– Richard F. Slager, MD.**
**Past Vice President of Rotary International**

\* \* \* \* \*

As a lifelong salesman, I have learned not to ask for a check until the product is explained and sold. Perhaps we tend to skip over the "selling" part when we ask our fellow members to support The Rotary Foundation. It is a "product" that has great value and can certainly sell itself with our help.

- How do you calculate the value of a lifetime of goodwill emanating from the visit of a GSE team after they return to their own country?

- How do you measure the impact of an Ambassadorial Scholar who has experienced Rotary generosity first hand?

- What is the value of a life saved from the crippling effects of Polio because a child was taken to a National Immunization Day site and given the two drops of vaccine on his tongue by a man or woman wearing a yellow vest with the Rotary emblem on it?

- Or a matching grant to provide food for starving people in Zimbabwe?

- Or of free cataract surgery to restore sight to thousands of blind poor people in India?

- Or providing a sewing machine to a poor woman allowing her to have her own business in Turkey?

- Or a clean-water well in a Nicaraguan community?

- What is the impact in your district when a member returns from being a Rotary Volunteer in another country and relates what he/she has seen?

Linda and I took our 15-year-old grandson, Jonathan, with us to India where we have a decade-long relationship with a cataract surgery program in Kanpur. Dr. Awadh Dubey has done thousands of free cataract surgeries for poor blind people. As we all took a nighttime train journey to the holy city of Varinasi, Dr. Dubey and Jonathan talked for a long time. Later, the doctor said to me, "This trip will change your grandson's life." The next year, Dr. Dubey and his wife were our guests in Indiana (District 6560) where he was the main speaker at our district conference. Our grandson was in the audience as the doctor described his philanthropic work with the aide of a visual presentation. After the speech, Jonathan asked his mother if he could take money out of his savings account to contribute to our Vision for the Future fund, which supports that work. Jonathan had seen the "product" and was sold on it enough to write a check.

> "I will let you in on a secret. There is sufficient money in Rotary to fund every program that the imagination of Rotarians can come up with. The problem is it's still in the pockets of Rotarians. How do we unlock those purses and wallets?"
> – Allan Jagger, Rotary International Training Leader at 2006 International Assembly

I once asked Rotary Foundation Trustee Kalyan Banerjee (who is from India) whether he thinks National Immunization Day volunteers are more trouble than they are worth to their members who must host us. Trustee Banerjee said all volunteers are welcome, are needed, and provide visual evidence that the rest of the world cares about their problems. Those same volunteers return home and become more "salesmen" for the good work of The Rotary Foundation.

If you have not been a Rotary Volunteer, think about it. If you cannot do so, you can be a part of this good work by contributing at least $100.00 every year to The Annual Programs Fund. With that contribution, you can support the volunteers and thus be present at every project in the world.

With your enthusiastic personal and financial support, The Rotary Foundation will continue to promote world peace and understanding.

Rotary service, whether as a volunteer or as a donor, is just a matter of priorities. My goal for Rotary is for it to be strong, to survive, and thrive long after I am gone.

To survive by my help in building its membership.

To thrive by means of my help with Rotary's good work locally and around the world.

To give support with my physical involvement and with my checkbook.

Whether it is a work detail to pick up trash along a local highway, going on a National Immunization Day trip across the ocean, or writing a check every year, I can affirm my commitment to "Service Above Self." Supporting Rotary growth and Rotary causes is selfish, really, having something to do with wanting the work I consider important to continue. This will be a part of my legacy, when I am no longer here. I hope you support similar "selfish" priorities by contributing to our great Foundation.

– Tom Branum, Director,
Rotary International, 2006-2008;
Trustee, The Rotary Foundation 2002-2006.

\* \* \* \* \*

As I sift through my thoughts on this, my second Rotary humanitarian mission, I again realize that the power of what was accomplished was not in what we did, but in the foundation we laid for tomorrow.

During a mission like this there are so many tangible accomplishments: restored sight, installation of new medical equipment, improved water filtration and plumbing, or providing computers and books for a library. The intangible accomplishments, however, hold much greater hope for the future and potential value: the restored vision to a child that gives the capability to learn and then later to return to teach, the equipment that gives the physician the ability to better diagnose a malady and save lives, the sanitary water that improves the health of many, or the lessons learned from reading the thoughts of others. These are the accomplishments that build a better future for the world. One full of hope and one without fear of other cultures. One without hate. One without thinking the images seen on television and in the newspapers describe how people are. We will accomplish these tasks one at a time, little by little.

As Rotarians we touched everyone we met and worked with. We taught by our example to serve. We taught that we expect nothing in return except a willingness to learn and move forward. We taught that when we promise, we deliver.

Many friendships were developed during this mission, some within the team, many from the local community. Communication with many has continued and where it will lead, only time will tell. Personally, they will not be forgotten, sometimes the memories are stored away for use on another day to teach another lesson, others will forever remain a tear in my eye.

**– Mark Warchol, West York Rotary Club (District 7390) after returning from his third volunteer trip to a Rotary Foundation project**

\* \* \* \* \*

"By the time the world is certified polio-free, Rotary's contributions to the global polio eradication effort will exceed US$600 million. In addition, millions of dollars of 'in-kind" and personal contributions have been made by and through local Rotary clubs and districts for polio eradication activities. Of even greater significance has been the huge volunteer army mobilized by Rotary International. Hundreds of thousands of volunteers at the local level are providing support at clinics or mobilizing their communities for immunization or polio eradication activities. More than one million Rotarians worldwide have contributed toward the success of the polio eradication effort to date."[6]

---

[6] International PolioPlus Committee report, January 2006

\* \* \* \* \*

"From the launch of the global initiative in 1988, to the eradication target of 2005, 5 million people, mainly in the developing world, who would otherwise have been paralyzed, will be walking because they have been immunized against polio. More than 500,000 cases of polio are now prevented each year by the efforts of governments and the partnership of the World Health Organization (WHO), Rotary International, the United Nations Children's Fund (UNICEF), the United States Centers for Disease Control and Preventions (CDC), and the overseas development agencies of donor nations."[7]

\* \* \* \* \*

"As a result of the efforts of Rotary International and its Foundation and those of our partners, more than two billion children have [by 2005] received oral polio vaccine. Since 1998, the inclusion of Vitamin A supplements on NIDs has averted an estimated 1.25 million childhood deaths [from diseases such as River Blindness]. A child can be protected against polio for as little as US$0.60 worth of vaccine."[8]

\* \* \* \* \*

"Once polio has been eradicated, the world will reap substantial financial, as well as humanitarian, dividends due to foregone polio treatment and rehabilitation costs. Depending on national decisions on the future use of polio vaccines, these savings could exceed US$1 billion per year."[9]

---

[7] International PolioPlus Committee report, January 2006
[8] International PolioPlus Committee report, January 2006
[9] International PolioPlus Committee report, January 2006

\* \* \* \* \*

I often speak to the uniqueness of OUR FOUNDATION, particularly our humanitarian projects (matching grants) in that:

Rotarians design our humanitarian projects.

Rotarians work together to raise the dollars needed

Rotarians work together implementing the project directly and hands on

Rotarians advocate sustainable projects

Rotarians oversee TRF humanitarian projects and retain stewardship

or...

We plan

We participate

We pay for the project

We provide hands-on participation

We provide oversight and stewardship

We help achieve goodwill, better understanding, and peace.

Why we support the Rotary Foundation:

My wife Patti and I are immensely proud of Rotary's World Peace Fellowship Program and knowing that our endowment will live on in perpetuity and benefit generations of peace scholars in years to come is extremely gratifying.

We believe that leaving a legacy for future generations of Rotary World Peace Scholars is one of the greatest things we can do in our lives.

**– Dr. and Mrs. Edward "Eddie" Blender.**
**(Eddie is a Past District Governor in District 5470.)**

When farsighted Rotarians in District 5340 (California, USA) looked at the gamut of needs in post-Taliban Afghanistan, they had a clear vision for meeting one need that would help overcome many of the others—education.

Rotary Volunteer Fary Moini and PDG Steve Brown spearheaded an effort by their Rotary Club of La Jolla Golden Triangle that raised US $100,000 to establish a school in Jalalabad, Afghanistan. Other supporters included The Rotary Foundation of Rotary International with a grant for the equipment, the Afghan government, local Abdul Haq Foundation, and the U.S.-based Donner Foundation. The Rotary Club of Uni Town Peshawar, Pakistan, helped coordinate the project locally.

It was gratifying to see that over 50 percent of the students were girls," said Brown, who attended the inauguration of the Najmul Jahad Rotary School in March 2004. "This is really important, for girls had been previously banned from attending school. Education is so fundamental and these people have so little. The school is a symbol of hope for the future. All you had to do was look in the eyes of the kids."

Moini oversaw final development of the school, which will eventually enroll 2,000 students. She also taught English as a second language at a high school in Jalalabad, helped develop and install a satellite-based computer center at Nangarbar University as another project of her club, and provided other humanitarian service, all with the aid of a Foundation Individual Grant.

Another initiative, the Afghan Women's Development Center, was supported by the Rotary Club of Encinitas, California, and a Foundation Matching Grant. In addition, District 5340 Rotarians Steve Spencer and Farid Saydee are teaching in Afghanistan with the support of the Steve Brown Advised Fund as part of another Foundation program.

"It is clear that in the area of Afghanistan where we are working, Rotary is making a measurable difference in lives," said Brown. "We are doing things on the same or greater magnitude as (national) governments"

– Rotary Foundation annual report 2003-04

## Appendix B

# Useful Rotary Foundation Resources

The Rotary Foundation is a dynamic organization that strives to adapt to changing times. Programs, policies, and procedures might differ from those described in printed materials. For the most up-to-date information on the work of our Foundation, visit www.Rotary.org and click on the Rotary Foundation link.

**The Rotary Foundation Quick Reference Guide** (219-EN)
Pamphlet providing essential information on The Rotary Foundation's programs, grant-making requirements, and contribution recognition levels. Free

**Rotary Foundation Facts** (159-EN)
A brief statistical overview of the organization, scope, and programs of the Foundation. Free.

**The Rotary Foundation: The International Vision of Rotary** (065-EN)
A 15-minute documentary with footage from around the world that provides an inspirational overview of the Foundation's humanitarian and educational programs.

### The Rotary Foundation: Be a Part of It (131-EN)

An eight-minute video that features brief anecdotes about Group Study Exchange, Matching Grants, PolioPlus, and Rotary Foundation Scholarship programs.

### District Rotary Foundation Committee Manual (300-EN)

A resource manual designed for the district Rotary Foundation committee.

### Club Rotary Foundation Guide (155-EN)

Guide helps clubs organize their support for The Rotary Foundation and outlines the role of the club Rotary Foundation committee and the chair's responsibilities. Free

### GSE Team Poster (077-EN)

Color poster suitable for display, advertising the Group Study Exchange program of The Rotary Foundation, 18 x 24 in (46 x 61 cm). English only. US$3.

### Rotary Centers for International Studies PowerPoint (049-MU)

CD-ROM describes the Rotary Centers program: its history, objectives, funding, and application procedures. Suitable for Rotarians and nonmembers. Limited quantities per order. Free.

### Rotary Global Projects Footage (920-MU)

Footage and images from around the world that clubs and districts can use to enhance their own video stories of humanitarian service. Use these images to design your own videos for local TV stations. DVS data disc (will not work on a standard DVD player). $15.

### Rotary International, Humanity in Motion II (609-EN)

Second part of the global public image campaign focuses on Rotary's work to advance peace through its educational programs. Kit includes a CD-ROM containing ready-made print ads, Internet banners, and outdoor ad designs, and a DVD with two public service announcements for television, which clubs can use for local media placement. Free.

**Rotary Peace and Conflict Studies brochure** (105-EN)
Overview of short-term certificate peace studies program at
Chulalongkorn University in Bangkok, Thailand, includes course
features. Also available in Thai. Free

**Rotary World Peace Fellowships leaflet** (084-EN)
Revised two-color leaflet, suitable for display, provides potential
applicants and Rotarians with information about the objectives,
eligibility requirements, funding, and application process for the
Rotary World peace Fellowship and a description of the Rotary
Centers for International Studies. (Order together with 082 and
083). Limited quantities per order. Free

**RVM:** *The Rotarians* **Video Magazine, Volume 1, Issue 2**
(506-MU)
Second in a series of DVDs portraying the achievements and
projects of Rotarians worldwide. This edition features a profile of
Rotarian D'Lisa Simmons, hands-on techniques for teaching math
and science to U.S. schoolchildren, free dental care for Russian
orphans, safe haven for Thailand's hill tribe children, highlights
from the 2005 Rotary International Convention, and more. (English, with subtitles in FR, JA, KO, PO, SP), DVD, $15.

| | |
|---|---|
| 3-H | Health, Hunger and Humanitarian program |
| Ambassadorial Scholarships | Scholarships to students to study abroad. |
| Annual Programs Fund | Provide funding for The Rotary Foundation's programs. Contributions are invested for three years and then 50% is returned to the district as DDF and 50% supports humanitarian and GSE programs. |
| Arch Klumph Society | People who have contributed $250,000 or more to The Rotary Foundation |
| Benefactor | A person who makes provision for $1,000 or more to the Permanent Fund in their estate plan |
| Blane Community Grants | Up to $1,000 grants to help clubs & districts in the USA improve local immunization |
| DDF | District Designated Fund (also known as *SHARE* Fund). 50% of the amount the district contributed three years ago is now available for the district to allocate for Rotary Foundation grants or programs |
| District Simplified Grants | Up to 20% of its DDF may be used by the district for service projects or humanitarian programs |
| GSE | Group Study Exchange |
| SHARE System | See DDF above |

| | |
|---|---|
| Major Donor | Outright or accumulated contributions of $10,000 or above earn Major Donor status. |
| Matching Grants | The Foundation provides a 1:1 match of DDF and 0.5:1 match of cash contributions for eligible projects |
| Paul Harris Fellow | A $1,000 outright or accumulated donation earns recognition as a Paul Harris Fellow |
| Paul Harris Society | A person who contributes $1,000 each year |
| Permanent Fund | The endowment fund where only the earnings are used to fund Rotary Foundation programs |
| PolioPlus | The global campaign to eradicate polio |
| PolioPlus Partners | Campaign to fund polio immunization efforts, such as National Immunization Day costs |
| Rotary Centers for International Studies in Peace and Conflict Resolution | Seven centers at major universities around the world that offer one- and two-year graduate-level courses in peacemaking and conflict resolution |
| Rotary Foundation Alumni | The 85,000 people who have participated in scholarship, Rotary Volunteer, and GSE programs since 1945 |
| Sustaining Member | Person who gives at least $100 to the Foundation with the goal of ultimately reaching the $1,000 Paul Harris Fellow level |
| University Teachers grants | Grants to encourage university teachers to volunteer for 3-10 months in a low income country |

The global eradication of polio will leave a legacy of better health for children not only by ending a deadly, crippling disease but in many other ways, including:

- Potential global savings of more than US$1 billion per year with the eventual elimination of immunization, treatment, and rehabilitation expenses.

- Continued benefits from the World Health Organization's surveillance network, established with Rotary's help, which includes 140 laboratories worldwide. This infrastructure, created originally for the Polio Eradication Initiative, is now also being used to fight yellow fever, meningitis, cholera, measles, and other diseases.

- The PolioPlus program as a model of cooperation between nongovernmental organizations and government agencies on a large-scale public health initiative.

# Make *Frank Talk* work for your club and district

Tens of thousands of Rotarians the world over have used *Frank Talk* to tell the story of Rotary—and help bring in new members.

Many went on to buy *Frank Talk II* to show their members how to change with the times, do their part to energize their club, and make members more active and involved—and keep wavering members from leaving!

Now you can add *Frank Talk on Our Rotary Foundation* to their library! This valuable resource will educate Rotarians about the work of The Rotary Foundation and motivate them to be more supportive of your club and district Foundation goals...whether your objective is to increase Foundation giving, or to encourage greater participation in hands-on volunteer service.

## Look at how you can save money by ordering copies for each member.

|  | Frank Talk | Frank Talk 2 | Frank Talk 3 |  |
|---|---|---|---|---|
| Single copy | $12.95 | $12.95 | $12.95 |  |
| 10-24 copies | $ 7.95 | $ 7.95 | $ 7.95 | *Save 39%!* |
| 25-99 copies | $ 4.95 | $ 4.95 | $ 4.95 | *Save 62%!* |
| 100 or more copies* | $ 4.50* | $ 4.50* | $ 4.50* | *Save 65%!* |

*The three titles can be combined, in lots of 25, and still receive this rate for orders totaling 100 or more. Prices are in US$.

**To order:**
Call +1.856.988.1738
OR
Fax +1.856.988.0511
OR
Order online at our secure sites:
www.FrankTalkBooks.com or www.FrankDevlyn.org